Ready® Classroom
Mathematics

Grade 3 • Volume 2

Curriculum Associates®

978-1-4957-8037-0
©2020–Curriculum Associates, LLC
North Billerica, MA 01862
No part of this book may be reproduced
by any means without written permission
from the publisher.
All Rights Reserved. Printed in USA.
5 6 7 8 9 10 11 12 13 14 15   21 20

BTS20

Contents

UNIT 3

Multiplication
Finding Area, Solving Word Problems, and Using Scaled Graphs

Contents (continued)

UNIT 4

Fractions
Equivalence and Comparison, Measurement, and Data

$\frac{1}{8}$ mile

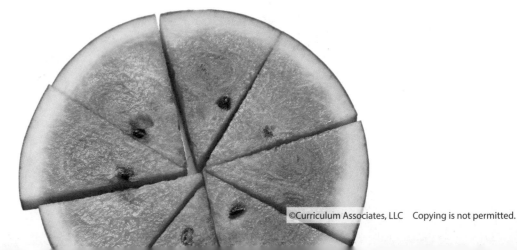

UNIT 5

Measurement
Time, Liquid Volume, and Mass

····· UNIT ·····
6
Shapes
Attributes and Categories, Perimeter and Area, and Partitioning

☑ SELF CHECK

Before starting this unit, check off the skills you know below. As you complete each lesson, see how many more skills you can check off!

I can . . .	Before	After
Use a fraction to show equal parts of a whole, for example: when a whole has 4 equal parts, each part is $\frac{1}{4}$ of the whole.	☐	☐
Use a number line to show fractions, and find a fraction on a number line.	☐	☐
Understand that equivalent fractions show the same amount and name the same point on a number line.	☐	☐
Find equivalent fractions, for example: fractions equivalent to $\frac{1}{2}$ include $\frac{2}{4}$, $\frac{3}{6}$, and $\frac{4}{8}$.	☐	☐
Write whole numbers as fractions, for example: $5 = \frac{5}{1}$ or $\frac{10}{2}$.	☐	☐
Compare fractions with the same numerator or the same denominator, including using $<$, $>$, and $=$, for example: $\frac{1}{3} > \frac{1}{8}$ and $\frac{4}{6} < \frac{5}{6}$.	☐	☐
Measure length to the nearest $\frac{1}{2}$ or $\frac{1}{4}$ inch and show data on a line plot.	☐	☐

Build Your Vocabulary

Math Vocabulary

Label the illustrations with a review fraction word. Then compare and discuss your answers with your partner.

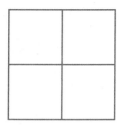  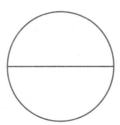 

....

Work with your teacher to complete the sentence frames below using the compare review words.

88 is .... 81.

56 is .... 61.

Academic Vocabulary

Put a check next to the academic words you know. Then use the words to complete the sentences.

☐ decide   ☐ label   ☐ point out   ☐ however

1 I would like to .... that the shape is divided into three equal parts.

2 He thought the shape was divided into fourths, ... , when he looked again, he realized it was divided into thirds.

3 I will .... an illustration of a cube by writing the word *cube* under it.

4 When you solve problems, you can .... what strategies to use to help solve them.

Understand What a Fraction Is

Dear Family,

This week your child is exploring what a fraction is.

Fractions are numbers that describe equal parts of a whole. The bottom number in a fraction is the **denominator**. It tells how many equal parts are in the whole. The top number in a fraction is the **numerator**. It tells how many parts are being described.

$\frac{1}{2}$, or one half, of this rectangle has been shaded.

 $\dfrac{\text{1 part shaded}}{\text{2 equal parts in the whole}}$

$\frac{1}{2}$ is a **unit fraction** because it names just one equal part of a whole.

$\frac{1}{3}$, or one third, is another example of a unit fraction.

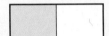

Two $\frac{1}{3}$ s of the rectangle below have been shaded. So, you write that $\frac{2}{3}$, or two thirds, is shaded.

Invite your child to share what he or she knows about what a fraction is by doing the following activity together.

ACTIVITY SAY AND WRITE FRACTIONS

Do this activity with your child to understand what a fraction is.

Materials pencil and paper, assorted items to divide, scissors or knife

Help your child become familiar with writing fractions by doing this activity together.

- Find at least three "whole" items in your house that can be divided into equal parts. Some examples are a sandwich, an apple, or a sheet of paper.

- Work together to show equal parts. For example, cut a sandwich into 4 parts that are the same size or divide the paper into 8 equal parts.

- Then take turns saying and writing a fraction and then showing that fraction of the object. For example, if one person says "one fourth" and writes "$\frac{1}{4}$," the other person points to 1 part of the sandwich. If one person says "three eighths" and writes "$\frac{3}{8}$," the other person points to 3 parts of the paper.

- Use fractions with denominators of 2, 3, 4, 6, and 8.

Explore What a Fraction Is

How can you describe equal parts?

Learning Target
• Understand a fraction $\frac{1}{b}$ as the quantity formed by 1 part when a whole is partitioned into b equal parts; understand a fraction $\frac{a}{b}$ as the quantity formed by a parts of size $\frac{1}{b}$.

SMP 1, 2, 3, 4, 5, 6

MODEL IT

Complete the problems below.

1 **Fractions** are numbers that tell about equal parts of a whole.

a. Circle all the shapes that show one third shaded.

b. How do you know you circled the right shapes in Part a?

2 There are two numbers to a fraction. The bottom number, the **denominator**, tells how many equal parts are in the whole. The top number, the **numerator**, tells how many equal parts are being described. Write the fraction for the shaded part of the shapes you circled in problem 1.

$$\frac{\text{parts shaded} \longrightarrow \boxed{}}{\text{parts in the whole} \longrightarrow \boxed{}}$$

3 You write or name the fraction $\frac{1}{3}$ in words as "one third."

a. How would you write the fraction $\frac{1}{4}$ in words?

b. How would you write the fraction $\frac{1}{2}$ in words?

DISCUSS IT

• Did you and your partner use the same words to name the fractions in problem 3?

• I think you can use words or a number to name a fraction because . . .

MODEL IT

Complete the problems below.

4 A **unit fraction** has a 1 in the numerator. It names 1 part of a whole. Shade $\frac{1}{4}$ of the model below.

5 Look at the same model again.

a. Shade three fourths of the model.

b. How could you count each fourth you shaded to also name the fraction? Fill in the missing fourths.

1 fourth, ... fourths, ... fourths

c. Write the fraction for the parts you shaded in Part a.

$$\frac{\text{parts shaded} \longrightarrow \boxed{}}{\text{parts in the whole} \longrightarrow \boxed{}}$$

d. How would you name the fraction from Part c in words?

DISCUSS IT

• Count by $\frac{1}{4}$ s up to one whole. How do you know when to stop?

• I think counting by $\frac{1}{4}$ s is like counting whole numbers because . . .

• I think counting by $\frac{1}{4}$ s is different from counting whole numbers because . . .

6 REFLECT

Explain why the denominator does not change when you are counting by the unit fraction $\frac{1}{4}$ to reach $\frac{3}{4}$.

....

....

....

Prepare for Exploring What a Fraction Is

1 Think about what you know about fractions. Fill in each box. Use words, numbers, and pictures. Show as many ideas as you can.

Word	In My Own Words	Example
fraction		
numerator		
denominator		

2 Shade two thirds of the model. Write the fraction for the parts you shaded.

$$\frac{\text{parts shaded}}{\text{parts in the whole}} \longrightarrow \frac{\square}{\square}$$

Solve.

3 Circle all the shapes that show one fourth shaded. How do you know you circled the right shapes?

Solution ....

....

....

4 Write the fraction for the shaded part of the shapes you circled in problem 3.

$$\frac{\text{parts shaded} \longrightarrow \boxed{}}{\text{parts in the whole} \longrightarrow \boxed{}}$$

5 How would you write the fraction $\frac{2}{4}$ in words?

Solution ....

Develop Describing Parts of a Whole with Fractions

MODEL IT: WRITE FRACTIONS FROM MODELS

Try these problems.

 a. What unit fraction is shown?

b. Shade 2 parts of the model. What fraction of the square did you shade?

....

 a. What unit fraction is shown?

b. Shade 6 parts of the model. What fraction of the circle did you shade?

....

 Write the fraction of the figure that is shaded. The parts in each model are all equal.

a.

b.

....

DISCUSS IT

• How did you know what fractions to write in problem 3?

• I think shading equal parts of a figure shows a fraction because . . .

MODEL IT: DRAW MODELS OF FRACTIONS

Draw the figure described.

4 The model below shows $\frac{1}{3}$ of a square. Draw to show the whole square. Then shade to show $\frac{2}{3}$.

DISCUSS IT

- Did you and your partner draw the same figures for problems 4 and 5? Is there more than one correct answer for each problem?

5 The model below shows $\frac{1}{4}$ of a rectangle. Draw to show what the whole rectangle could look like. Then shade to show $\frac{2}{4}$.

- I think you need to know what the unit fraction piece of a model looks like to draw the rest of the model because . . .

CONNECT IT

Complete the problems below.

6 How can you use a shaded model to name a fraction?

7 Look at the rectangle.

a. What unit fraction is each part?

....

b. Shade 4 parts of the rectangle and write the fraction you shaded.

....

Practice Describing Parts of a Whole with Fractions

**Study how the Example shows how to write a fraction for parts of a whole.
Then solve problems 1–8.**

EXAMPLE

- There are 6 equal parts.

- Each part is one sixth, or $\frac{1}{6}$.

- 5 parts are shaded.

- Five sixths of the whole is shaded.

- This model shows the fraction $\frac{5}{6}$.

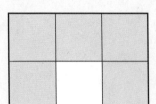

Fill in the blanks to describe each shape in problems 1 and 2.

 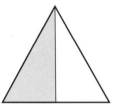

equal parts: ....

shaded part(s): ....

fraction of the whole that is shaded: ....

 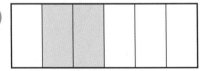

equal parts: ....

shaded part(s): ....

fraction of the whole that is shaded: ....

> **Vocabulary**
>
> **fraction** a number that names equal parts of a whole.

Solve.

3 Shade this shape to show $\frac{3}{4}$.

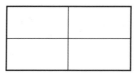

4 Shade this shape to show $\frac{2}{6}$.

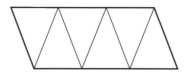

5 Shade 3 parts of this shape.

What fraction is shaded? ....

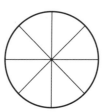

6 Shade 7 parts of this shape.

What fraction is shaded? ....

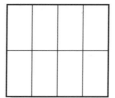

7 ▯ is $\frac{1}{4}$ of a rectangle.

Draw the rectangle. Show the parts.

8 ◺ is $\frac{1}{4}$ of a rectangle.

Draw the rectangle. Show the parts.
Then shade $\frac{2}{4}$ of your rectangle.

Refine Ideas About What a Fraction Is

APPLY IT
Complete these problems on your own.

1 CREATE

The part shown is $\frac{1}{6}$ of a rectangle. Draw a model to show what the whole rectangle might look like.

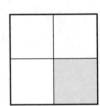

2 EXPLAIN

Look at these squares. Each is divided into equal parts.

Lynn says each square has the same fraction shaded. Rose says each square has a different fraction shaded. Explain who is correct and why.

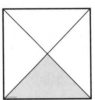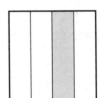

3 COMPARE

Look at these triangles. Each is divided into equal parts.

What is the same about the fraction of each model that is shaded?

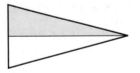

What is different about the fraction of each model that is shaded?

PAIR/SHARE
Discuss your solutions for these three problems with a partner.

Use what you have learned to complete problem 4.

4 Adam has $\frac{1}{3}$ of a pizza, Hillary has $\frac{2}{6}$ of a pizza, and John has $\frac{3}{8}$ of a pizza.

Adam

Hillary

John

Part A Show the number of equal parts in each pizza. Then shade each pizza to show the fraction each person has.

Part B Circle one of the pizzas. Explain how you knew how many equal parts to show and how many parts to shade.

5 MATH JOURNAL

Mike has a circle divided into equal parts. One part is shaded, and the other three parts are not. Mike says his circle shows the fraction $\frac{1}{3}$. Is he correct? Draw a picture to help you explain.

Understand Fractions on a Number Line

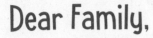

Dear Family,

This week your child is exploring fractions on a number line.

Fractions are numbers that name part of a whole. You can count fractions on a number line just like you can count whole numbers.

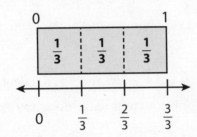

Number lines can also show fractions greater than 1. Each section between a pair of whole numbers (such as 0 and 1 or 1 and 2) can be cut into the same number of equal parts.

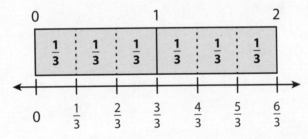

The number line above shows that 1 whole is the same as $\frac{3}{3}$ and that 2 wholes is the same as $\frac{6}{3}$.

On the number line below, the fraction at B is $\frac{5}{2}$. You can tell because each whole has been cut into halves. Counting by halves $\left(\frac{1}{2}\right)$, 1 whole is 2 halves, and 2 wholes is 4 halves. B marks the fifth half, which you write as $\frac{5}{2}$.

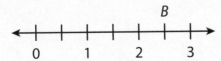

Invite your child to share what he or she knows about fractions on a number line by doing the following activity together.

ACTIVITY FRACTIONS ON A NUMBER LINE

Do this activity with your child to understand fractions on a number line.

Materials 2 number cubes with numbers 1–6, blank number lines below, pencils

Give your child practice finding fractions on a number line with this activity.

- Take turns rolling the number cubes. The sum of the two numbers on the cubes tells the numerator of your fraction. The denominator in this activity will always be 8. The number lines below are already marked in eighths for you.

- On your turn, find and mark the fraction on your number line and say the name of the fraction.

  For example, if the cubes rolled show 5 and 4, add 5 and 4 to get your numerator of 9. Then find and mark $\frac{9}{8}$ on your number line and say aloud: *My fraction is nine eighths*.

- If you get the same numerator again on another turn, you skip your turn.

- The first player to label five different fractions wins.

Player 1

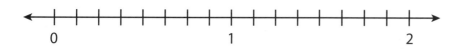

Player 2

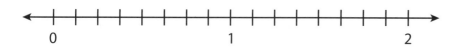

Explore **Fractions on a Number Line**

How can number lines help you understand fractions?

MODEL IT

Complete the models below.

1 This number line shows whole numbers. The distance from each number to the next is 1 whole. Complete the number line by filling in the missing number labels.

1 whole	1 whole	1 whole

0

....

2 Fractions are numbers that name parts of a whole. You can show fractions on a number line. On the number line below, the whole that is between 0 and 1 is divided into equal parts. Label each part of the area model with the unit fraction it represents.

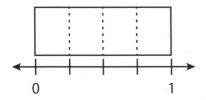

0   1

DISCUSS IT

- Did you and your partner label the parts the same way for problem 2?

- I think number lines can show fractions as well as whole numbers because . . .

MODEL IT
Complete the problems below.

3 You can count fractions on a number line just like you can count whole numbers.

a. Fill in the blanks to count the fourths below.

1, 2, 3, 4, . . .

1 fourth, ... fourths, ... fourths, ... fourths, . . .

b. Now count the fourths on the number line. Finish labeling the number line by filling in the missing numerators.

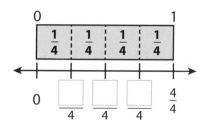

4 You can also use number lines to show fractions greater than 1. Complete the number line below by filling in the missing fraction labels.

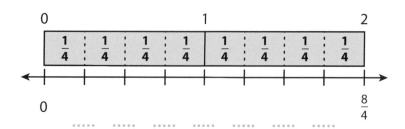

DISCUSS IT
- Did you and your partner use the same fractions to label the number line in problem 4?
- I think counting fractions is like counting whole numbers because . . .

Some fractions greater than 1 have a whole-number part and a fractional part. This is called a **mixed number**. Look at the fraction you labeled as $\frac{5}{4}$ on the number line above. Since $\frac{4}{4}$ is 1 whole, $\frac{5}{4}$ is the same as 1 whole and $\frac{1}{4}$ more. You can write this as the mixed number $1\frac{1}{4}$. 1 is the whole-number part and $\frac{1}{4}$ is the fractional part of the number.

5 REFLECT

Look at the fractions on the number line in problem 4. Why do you think the numerator and denominator are the same in the fraction that names 1 whole?

....

....

....

Prepare for Exploring Fractions on a Number Line

1 Think about what you know about fractions. Fill in each box. Use words, numbers, and pictures. Show as many ideas as you can.

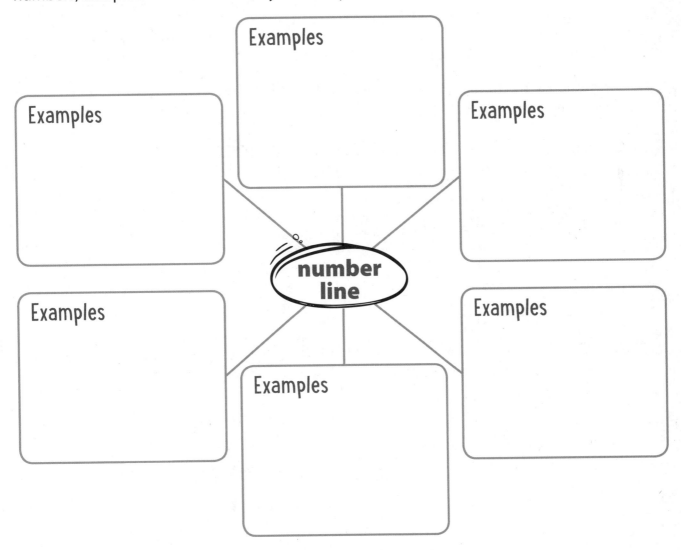

Examples

Examples

Examples

Examples

Examples

Examples

number line

2 On the number line below, the whole that is between 0 and 1 is divided into equal parts. Label each part of the area model with the unit fraction it represents.

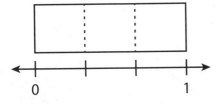

Lesson 21 Understand Fractions on a Number Line   **473**

Solve.

3 You can count fractions on a number line just like you can count whole numbers.

a. Fill in the blanks to count the thirds below.

1, 2, 3, . . .

1 third, ... thirds, ... thirds, . . .

b. Now count the thirds on the number line. Finish labeling the number line by filling in the missing numerators.

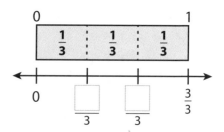

4 You can also use number lines to show fractions greater than 1. Complete the number line below by filling in the missing fraction labels.

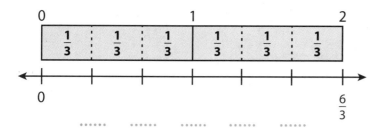

5 Look at the fractions on the number line in problem 4. Why do you think the numerator is twice the denominator in the fraction that names 2 wholes?

Solution ....

....

....

....

Develop Understanding of Fractions on a Number Line

MODEL IT: AREA MODELS

Try these two problems.

1 Write the missing labels on the number line under the area model.
Then tell what fraction each part of the area model shows.

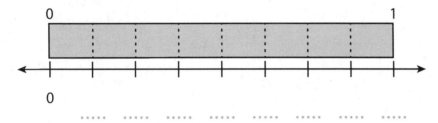

Each part shows ....

2 Write the missing labels on the number line under the area model.
Then tell what fraction each part of the area model shows.

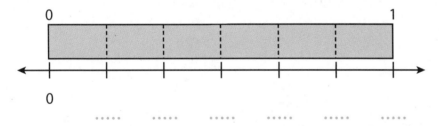

Each part shows ....

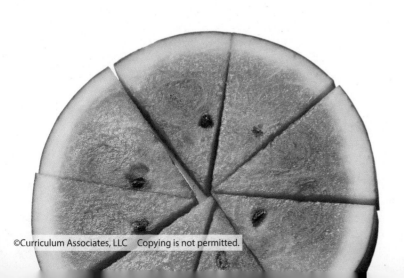

©Curriculum Associates, LLC   Copying is not permitted.

DISCUSS IT

• How did you decide what
the denominator was in
each problem?

• I think using an area model
helps me label fractions on
a number line because . . .

MODEL IT: NUMBER LINES

Identify the fraction at *A* on each number line.

3

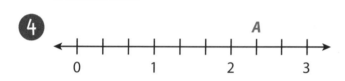

4

DISCUSS IT

• Did you and your partner use the same reasoning to answer problems 3 and 4?

• I think counting by unit fractions can help you identify the fractions in problems 3 and 4 because . . .

CONNECT IT

Complete the problems below.

5 How is using a number line to show fractions like using an area model? How is it different?

6 Use a number line to show the fraction.

a. $\frac{4}{6}$

b. $\frac{6}{4}$

Practice Showing Fractions on a Number Line

Study how the Example shows fractions on a number line.
Then solve problems 1–12.

EXAMPLE

The number line shows the section from 0 to 1.

The area model shows one whole.

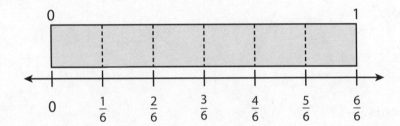

There are 6 equal parts in this section.

Each part is $\frac{1}{6}$ of the whole.

To label the marks, count like you do with whole numbers.

Use the area model and number line below to solve problems 1–4.

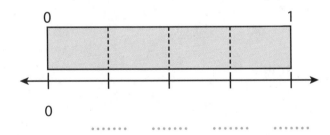

1 How many equal parts are there in this whole? ....

2 What fraction does each part show? ....

3 Label the marks on the number line.

4 What is another name for 1? ....

> **Vocabulary**
>
> **fraction** a number that names equal parts of a whole.

Use this number line to solve problems 5–8.

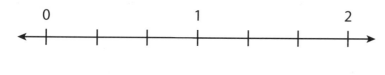

5 How many equal parts are between 0 and 1? ....

6 How many equal parts are between 1 and 2? ....

7 What fraction does each part show? ....

8 Write fractions to label the marks.

Use this number line to solve problems 9–11.

9 *A* is ....

10 *B* is ....

11 *C* is ....

12 Write the fraction $\frac{3}{2}$ where it belongs on this number line.

Explain how you knew where to put $\frac{3}{2}$.

Refine Ideas About Fractions on a Number Line

APPLY IT

Complete these problems on your own.

1 EXPLAIN

Amira says that A is at $\frac{7}{8}$.

Is she right? Explain.

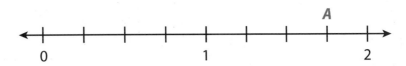

2 DEMONSTRATE

Use the number line below to show the fraction $\frac{5}{6}$.

Explain how you knew where to label $\frac{5}{6}$.

3 ILLUSTRATE

Use the number line below to show that there are 8 eighths in 1 whole.

PAIR/SHARE
Discuss your solutions for these three problems with a partner.

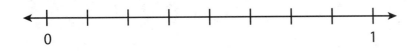

Lesson 21 Understand Fractions on a Number Line

Use what you have learned to complete problem 4.

4 Zara and John are hiking on a trail that is 2 miles long. There are signs to mark each eighth of a mile along the trail.

Part A Draw a number line to show the length of the trail. Then mark the number line off to show where each sign is.

Part B Zara stops for water at the $\frac{3}{8}$-mile sign. John stops to rest after $\frac{12}{8}$ miles. Label the $\frac{3}{8}$ mark on your number line with a Z for Zara and label the $\frac{12}{8}$ mark with a J for John.

Part C Who stops before the 1-mile mark? Who stops after the 1-mile mark? Explain how you know.

5 MATH JOURNAL

Explain how to show $\frac{3}{4}$ on a number line. Use a drawing to help.

Understand Equivalent Fractions

LESSON 22

Dear Family,

This week your child is exploring equivalent fractions.

Equivalent fractions show the same amount of the whole and name the same number, but they represent wholes that are cut into different numbers of equal-sized pieces.

To cover the same amount as $\frac{1}{2}$ of a whole, you need two $\frac{1}{4}$ s or three $\frac{1}{6}$ s or four $\frac{1}{8}$ s.

The diagram shows that:

$\frac{1}{2}$ and $\frac{2}{4}$ are equivalent fractions.

$\frac{1}{2}$ and $\frac{3}{6}$ are equivalent fractions.

$\frac{2}{4}$ and $\frac{4}{8}$ are equivalent fractions.

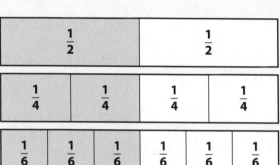

You can also show equivalent fractions using number lines. $\frac{1}{2}$ and $\frac{2}{4}$ are located at the same point on the number line, so they are equivalent.

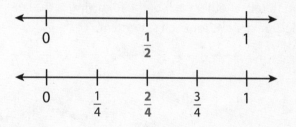

Notice that when talking about equivalent fractions, you must refer to a same-sized whole. The rectangles here are not the same size. They show that $\frac{1}{2}$ of a small rectangle is NOT equivalent to $\frac{2}{4}$ of a larger one.

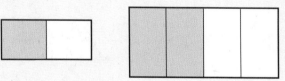

Invite your child to share what he or she knows about equivalent fractions by doing the following activity together.

ACTIVITY   MAKE FRACTION BARS

Do this activity with your child to understand equivalent fractions.

Materials paper, pencil, scissors

Explore equivalent fractions with your child with homemade fraction bars.

- Work together with your child to cut a regular sheet of paper into three strips lengthwise, each about 2 inches wide. The strips must be the same size.

- Fold one strip or bar in half to make two parts that are the same size.

- Fold the second bar in half and then in half again to make four parts that are all the same size.

- Fold the last bar in half three times to make eight equal parts.

- Unfold each bar. Draw lines on the fold lines and then label the sections. The sections of the first bar should be labeled $\frac{1}{2}$, the second bar $\frac{1}{4}$, and the last bar $\frac{1}{8}$.

- Now, lay the bars next to each other so the longest sides are touching. Use them to tell whether each of the following is true or false. Work together to circle *True* or *False* for each statement.

1. $\frac{1}{4} = \frac{2}{8}$ True   False

2. $\frac{3}{4} = \frac{3}{8}$ True   False

3. $\frac{1}{2} = \frac{4}{8}$ True   False

4. $\frac{2}{2} = \frac{4}{4}$ True   False

5. $\frac{2}{2} = \frac{2}{4}$ True   False

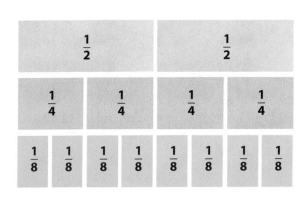

Answers: **1.** True; **2.** False; **3.** True; **4.** True; **5.** False

Explore Equivalent Fractions

How can two different fractions be equal?

Learning Target
• Understand two fractions as equivalent (equal) if they are the same size, or the same point on a number line.
SMP 1, 2, 3, 4, 5, 6, 7

MODEL IT

Complete the problems below.

1 The two circles and two number lines shown are the same size.

a. Shade $\frac{1}{2}$ of the first circle and $\frac{2}{4}$ of the second circle.

b. Label $\frac{1}{2}$ on the top number line and $\frac{2}{4}$ on the bottom number line.

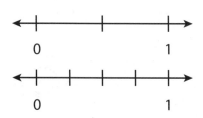

c. What can you say about the fractions $\frac{1}{2}$ and $\frac{2}{4}$?

2 Different fractions that name the same amount of the whole are **equivalent fractions**.

a. Circle the pair of models that shows that $\frac{1}{2}$ and $\frac{2}{4}$ are equivalent.

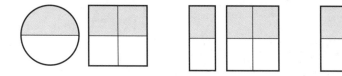

b. How did you know which pair of models to circle in Part a?

DISCUSS IT

• How do the number lines in problem 1 show that $\frac{1}{2}$ is equivalent to $\frac{2}{4}$?

• I think the wholes need to be the same size to compare fractions because . . .

MODEL IT

Complete the problems below.

3 Once you make sure the wholes are the same size, look at the size of the parts in each whole to name equivalent fractions.

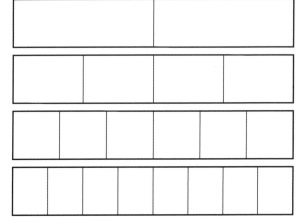

a. Label each part of the models at the right with the unit fraction it represents.

b. Shade the top model to show $\frac{1}{2}$. How many parts did you shade? ....

c. Shade the second model to show a fraction equivalent to $\frac{1}{2}$. How many parts did you shade? ....

d. Shade the third model to show a fraction equivalent to $\frac{1}{2}$. How many parts did you shade? ....

e. Shade the last model to show a fraction equivalent to $\frac{1}{2}$. How many parts did you shade? ....

f. Complete the equation using the models:

$$\frac{1}{2} = \frac{\boxed{}}{4} = \frac{\boxed{}}{6} = \frac{\boxed{}}{8}$$

DISCUSS IT

- Did you and your partner complete problem 3 the same way?

- I think $\frac{1}{2}$ is the largest unit fraction above because . . .

4 **REFLECT**

Explain why it takes more $\frac{1}{8}$s than $\frac{1}{4}$s to make a fraction equivalent to $\frac{1}{2}$.

....

....

....

Prepare for Exploring Equivalent Fractions

1 Think about what you know about fractions. Fill in each box. Use words, numbers, and pictures. Show as many ideas as you can.

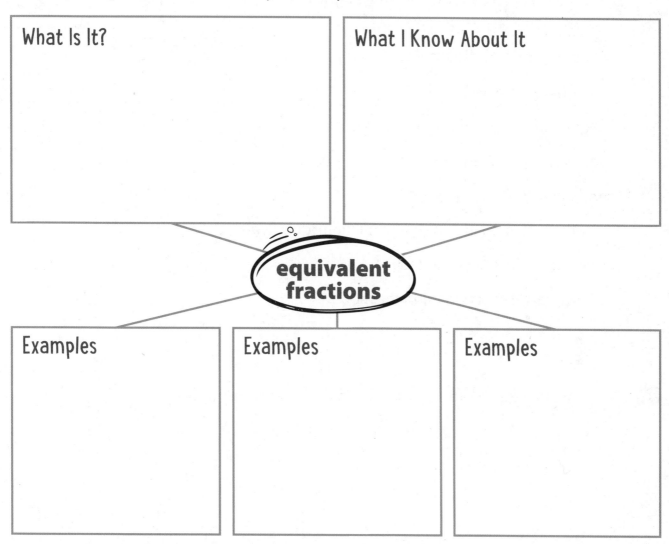

What Is It?	What I Know About It

equivalent fractions

Examples	Examples	Examples

2 Circle the pair of models that shows that $\frac{1}{2}$ and $\frac{3}{6}$ are equivalent. Explain.

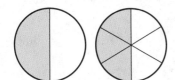 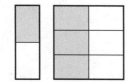 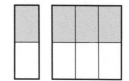

Solve.

3 Once you make sure the wholes are the same size, look at the size of the parts in each whole to name equivalent fractions.

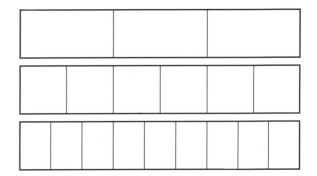

a. Label each part of the models at the right with the unit fraction it represents.

b. Shade the first model to show $\frac{1}{3}$. How many

parts did you shade? ....

c. Shade the second model to show a fraction

equivalent to $\frac{1}{3}$. How many parts did

you shade? ....

d. Shade the third model to show a fraction equivalent to $\frac{1}{3}$.

How many parts did you shade? ....

e. Complete the equation using the models:

$$\frac{1}{3} = \frac{\square}{6} = \frac{\square}{9}$$

4 Explain why it takes more $\frac{1}{9}$s than $\frac{1}{6}$s to make a fraction equivalent to $\frac{1}{3}$.

Develop Understanding of Equivalent Fractions

MODEL IT: NUMBER LINES

Try these two problems.

 a. Complete the number lines by writing the missing fractions.

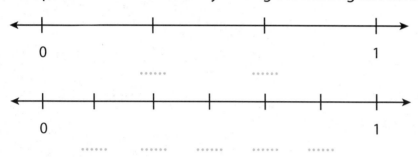

b. Write the equivalent fractions.

$\frac{1}{3} =$ ....

$\frac{2}{3} =$ ....

2 **a.** Complete the number lines by writing the missing fractions.

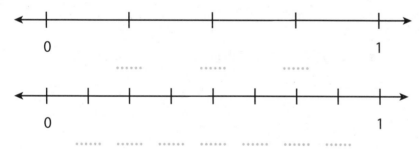

b. Write the equivalent fractions.

$\frac{1}{4} =$ ....

$\frac{6}{8} =$ ....

DISCUSS IT

• Did you and your partner complete the number lines the same way?

• I think number lines are a good way to show equivalent fractions because . . .

MODEL IT: FRACTION BARS

Use the fraction bars to show equivalent fractions.

3 Shade an amount equivalent to $\frac{2}{3}$ on the bottom bar.

$\frac{1}{3}$	$\frac{1}{3}$	$\frac{1}{3}$

$\frac{1}{6}$	$\frac{1}{6}$	$\frac{1}{6}$	$\frac{1}{6}$	$\frac{1}{6}$	$\frac{1}{6}$

What fraction did you shade? ....

4 Shade an amount equivalent to $\frac{4}{8}$ on the bottom bar.

$\frac{1}{8}$	$\frac{1}{8}$	$\frac{1}{8}$	$\frac{1}{8}$	$\frac{1}{8}$	$\frac{1}{8}$	$\frac{1}{8}$	$\frac{1}{8}$

$\frac{1}{6}$	$\frac{1}{6}$	$\frac{1}{6}$	$\frac{1}{6}$	$\frac{1}{6}$	$\frac{1}{6}$

What fraction did you shade? ....

DISCUSS IT

- Did you and your partner shade the fraction bars in the same way?

- I think fraction bars are a good way to show equivalent fractions because . . .

CONNECT IT

Complete the problems below.

5 How are fraction bars and number lines alike in showing equivalent fractions?

6 Label the number lines. Then list any equivalent fractions.

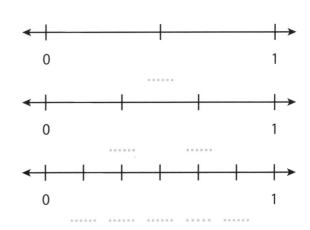

Practice Showing Equivalent Fractions

Study how the Example shows equivalent fractions with number lines and area models. Then solve problems 1–5.

EXAMPLE

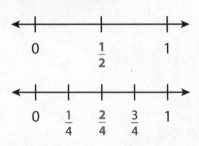

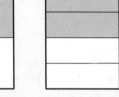

$\frac{1}{2}$ and $\frac{2}{4}$ are at the same place on the number lines.

$\frac{1}{2}$ is equivalent to $\frac{2}{4}$.

The rectangles have the same amount of shading.

$\frac{1}{2}$ is equivalent to $\frac{2}{4}$.

1 Does each model show equivalent fractions?

	Yes	No
$\frac{1}{2}$ $\frac{1}{2}$ / $\frac{1}{8}$ $\frac{1}{8}$ $\frac{1}{8}$ $\frac{1}{8}$ $\frac{1}{8}$ $\frac{1}{8}$ $\frac{1}{8}$ $\frac{1}{8}$	Ⓐ	Ⓑ
 $\frac{1}{2}$ $\frac{2}{6}$	Ⓒ	Ⓓ

Vocabulary

equivalent fractions
fractions that name the same part of a whole.
$\frac{1}{2}$ and $\frac{2}{4}$ are equivalent.

Use the number lines to identify equivalent fractions in problems 2 and 3.

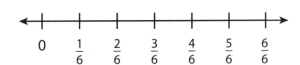

2 $\frac{2}{6} = $ ....

3 $\frac{2}{3} = $ ....

4 Look at the fractions shown by the shaded hexagons. Write equivalent fractions for the shaded parts.

$\frac{\square}{\square} = \frac{\square}{\square}$

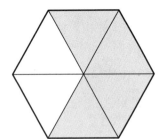
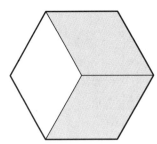

5 Shade $\frac{6}{8}$ of rectangle A. Then shade rectangle B to show a fraction equivalent to $\frac{6}{8}$.

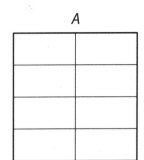

A   B

Write the equivalent fraction. ....

Refine Ideas About Equivalent Fractions

APPLY IT
Complete these problems on your own.

1 DEMONSTRATE

Use the fraction bars below to show $\frac{1}{4} = \frac{2}{8}$.

$\frac{1}{4}$	$\frac{1}{4}$	$\frac{1}{4}$	$\frac{1}{4}$

$\frac{1}{8}$	$\frac{1}{8}$	$\frac{1}{8}$	$\frac{1}{8}$	$\frac{1}{8}$	$\frac{1}{8}$	$\frac{1}{8}$	$\frac{1}{8}$

2 EXPLAIN

Cooper drew these models.
He says they show $\frac{2}{3} = \frac{2}{6}$.
What did Cooper do wrong?

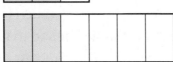

3 ILLUSTRATE

Draw marks on the number line below to show eighths. Above
each mark you make, write the fraction it shows.

0                          $\frac{1}{2}$ 1

PAIR/SHARE
Discuss your solutions for
these three problems with
a partner.

Which eighth is equivalent to $\frac{1}{2}$? ....

Use what you have learned to complete problem 4.

4 Four friends each ate a part of their own granola bar. All the granola bars were the same size. Meg ate $\frac{4}{6}$, Joe ate $\frac{4}{8}$, Beth ate $\frac{6}{8}$, and Amy ate $\frac{2}{3}$.

Part A Which two friends ate the same amount of a granola bar?

Complete the models to show that your answer is correct.

	Meg
	Joe
	Beth
	Amy

Part B Fred divided his granola bar into fourths. He ate the same amount as Beth. Label the number line to show how much Beth ate. Draw another number line for Fred's granola bar and mark how he divided his bar. Label the fraction of granola bar Fred ate.

What fraction of his granola bar did Fred eat? ....

Beth $\longleftarrow\!\!\!+\!\!+\!\!+\!\!+\!\!+\!\!+\!\!+\!\!+\!\!+\!\!\longrightarrow$

$\quad\quad 0 \quad \frac{1}{8} \quad \frac{2}{8} \quad \frac{3}{8} \quad \frac{4}{8} \quad \frac{5}{8} \quad \frac{6}{8} \quad \frac{7}{8} \quad 1$

5 MATH JOURNAL

When you draw two number lines to show equivalent fractions, how can you make sure that one whole is the same size on both number lines?

Find Equivalent Fractions

Dear Family,

This week your child is learning to find equivalent fractions.

Using a model or diagram to represent equivalent fractions helps make it clear why they are equivalent.

The models to the right show that $\frac{2}{8}$ and $\frac{1}{4}$ are equivalent because they cover the same amount of same-sized circles.

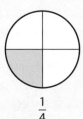

$\frac{1}{4}$

The circle showing $\frac{2}{8}$ has solid lines showing fourths and dotted lines showing how each fourth was cut to make eighths. It helps you see that since eighths are smaller than fourths, you need more of them to cover the same amount.

$\frac{2}{8}$

A number line is another model that can show equivalent fractions.

This number line shows both fourths and eighths. Since $\frac{1}{4}$ and $\frac{2}{8}$ are at the same point, $\frac{1}{4}$ and $\frac{2}{8}$ are equivalent.

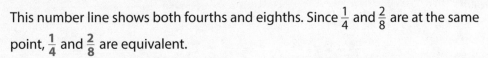

A whole number can be written as a fraction too, with a denominator of 1.

A denominator of 1 means the whole has not been cut into parts. One whole can be written $\frac{1}{1}$, 2 wholes as $\frac{2}{1}$, and so forth.

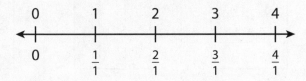

Invite your child to share what he or she knows about finding equivalent fractions by doing the following activity together.

ACTIVITY EQUIVALENT FRACTIONS

Do this activity with your child to recognize equivalent fractions.

Materials cards below, scissors

Play this matching game to practice recognizing equivalent fractions.

• Cut out the cards below and color the backs.

• Mix the cards and place them facedown in two rows.

• Take turns. On your turn, flip two cards. Name the fractions.

• If the cards show equivalent fractions, keep them. If they are not equivalent, turn them back over in the same places as before.

• When all the equivalent fractions have been found, the player with the most cards is the winner.

• As you play, ask your child questions such as:
  • *If you keep the cards, how do you know the fractions are equivalent?*
  • *If you turn the cards back over, how do you know the fractions are not equivalent?*

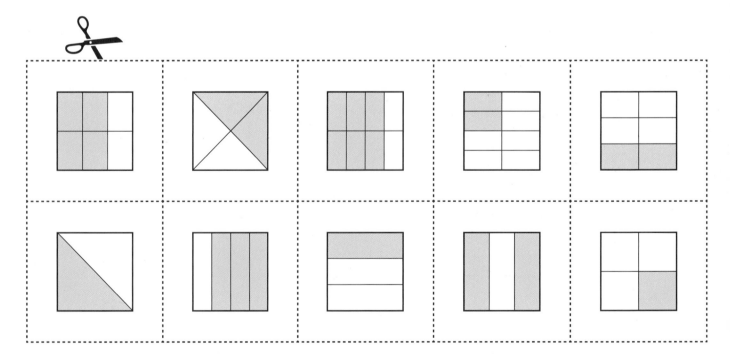

Explore Equivalent Fractions

Previously you learned that equivalent fractions name the same amount of the whole. In this lesson you will learn more about finding equivalent fractions. Use what you know to try to solve the problem below.

> **Izzy's mom bakes a cake. She puts chocolate frosting on half of the cake and vanilla frosting on half of the cake. Then Izzy's mom cuts the cake into fourths so that each fourth has either all chocolate or all vanilla frosting.**
>
> **What fraction other than $\frac{1}{2}$ names the part of the cake that has chocolate frosting?**

TRY IT

 Math Toolkit
- fraction circles
- 1-inch grid paper
- index cards
- crayons
- fraction models
- number lines

DISCUSS IT

Ask your partner: Can you explain that again?

Tell your partner: I knew . . . so I . . .

CONNECT IT

1 LOOK BACK

What fraction other than $\frac{1}{2}$ names the part of the cake that has chocolate

frosting? .... How did you get your answer?

2 LOOK AHEAD

You have seen many different types of fraction models, such as area models, number lines, and fractions bars. You can find equivalent fractions by dividing the same model in different ways.

a. Each cake below shows fourths. Draw lines on one of the cakes to show eighths.

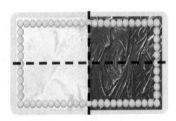      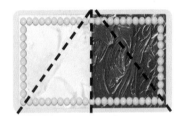

b. How many pieces of the cake have chocolate frosting now? ....

c. You can also look at different equal-sized parts on a number line to find equivalent fractions. Fill in the fraction for fourths that is equivalent to $\frac{1}{2}$.

3 REFLECT

Why does it make sense that $\frac{1}{2}$ and $\frac{2}{4}$ can name the same amount?

....

....

....

Prepare for Finding Equivalent Fractions

1 Think about what you know about fractions. Fill in each box. Use words, numbers, and pictures. Show as many ideas as you can.

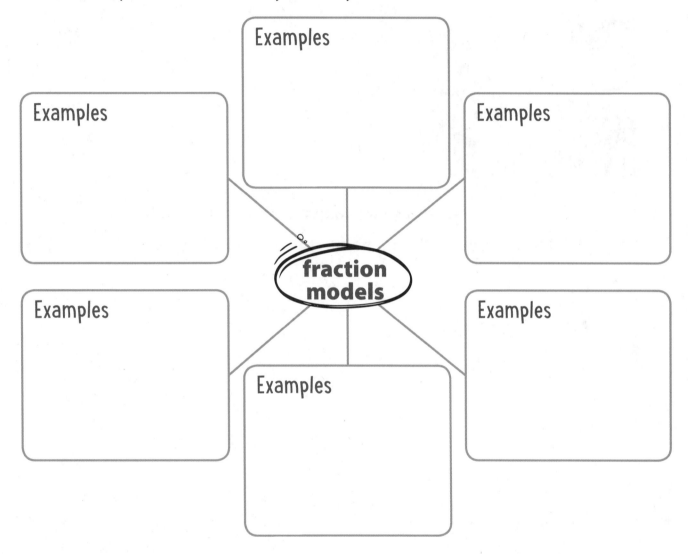

Examples

Examples

Examples

Examples

Examples

Examples

fraction models

2 Each fraction model below shows thirds. Draw lines on each model to show sixths.

 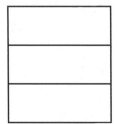 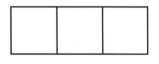

③ Solve the problem. Show your work.

Len has 3 strips of construction paper. Each strip is the same size and a different color—red, yellow, and pink. He tapes the strips together to make a rectangle.

Then Len divides the rectangle into sixths so that each sixth is one color. What fraction other than $\frac{1}{3}$ names the part of the rectangle that is red?

④ Check your answer. Show your work.

Develop Finding Equivalent Fractions

Read and try to solve the problem below.

> Carl eats $\frac{2}{8}$ of an orange. Trey's orange is the same size. He eats $\frac{1}{4}$ of it. Show that the two boys eat the same amount of an orange.

TRY IT

Math Toolkit
- fraction tiles
- fraction circles
- fraction models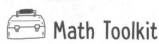
- number lines
- grid paper

DISCUSS IT

Ask your partner: How did you choose that strategy?

Tell your partner: A model I used was . . . It helped me . . .

Explore different ways to understand finding equivalent fractions.

Carl eats $\frac{2}{8}$ of an orange. Trey's orange is the same size. He eats $\frac{1}{4}$ of it. Show that the two boys eat the same amount of an orange.

PICTURE IT

You can use models to help find equivalent fractions.

This model shows $\frac{2}{8}$.

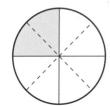

This model shows $\frac{1}{4}$.

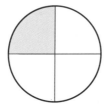

Look at the model of $\frac{2}{8}$. The solid lines divide the circle into fourths. The dashed lines divide each fourth in half to make eighths.

MODEL IT

You can also use a number line to help find equivalent fractions.

This number line shows both fourths and eighths.

$$0 \qquad \frac{1}{4} \qquad \frac{2}{4} \qquad \frac{3}{4} \qquad 1$$

$$0 \quad \frac{1}{8} \quad \frac{2}{8} \quad \frac{3}{8} \quad \frac{4}{8} \quad \frac{5}{8} \quad \frac{6}{8} \quad \frac{7}{8} \quad 1$$

CONNECT IT

Now you will use the problem from the previous page to help you understand how to find equivalent fractions.

1 Look at the models in **Picture It**. How do you know that $\frac{2}{8}$ of the first model is shaded?

2 How do you know that $\frac{1}{4}$ of the second model is shaded?

3 Explain how the models show that the fractions $\frac{2}{8}$ and $\frac{1}{4}$ are equivalent.

4 How does the number line in **Model It** show that the fractions $\frac{2}{8}$ and $\frac{1}{4}$ are equivalent?

5 Complete the sentences to show that the fractions of the two oranges name the same amount.

Use words: Two eighths is equal to ....

Use fractions: $\frac{2}{8} =$ ....

6 Describe two different ways to show two fractions are equivalent.

7 REFLECT

Look back at your **Try It**, strategies by classmates, and **Picture It** and **Model It**. Which models or strategies do you like best for finding equivalent fractions? Explain.

....

....

....

....

APPLY IT

Use what you just learned to solve these problems.

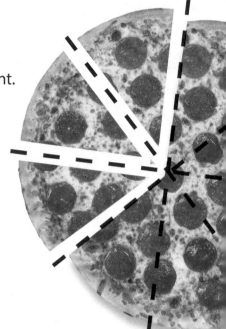

8 Lina and Adam each order a small pizza. They eat the same amount. Lina eats $\frac{3}{4}$ of her pizza. Adam's pizza is divided into 8 slices. How many slices of pizza did Adam eat? Show your work.

Solution ....

9 Draw a model to show $\frac{2}{3} = \frac{4}{6}$.

10 Use the number line to find a fraction equivalent to $\frac{1}{3}$.
Show your work.

Solution ....

Practice Finding Equivalent Fractions

**Study the Example showing how to find equivalent fractions.
Then solve problems 1–8.**

EXAMPLE

Maria colors $\frac{1}{3}$ of her art paper red. Erica colors $\frac{2}{6}$ of her art paper green. The papers are the same size. Do the two girls color the same amount of their art papers?

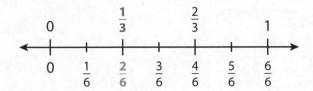

Maria colors $\frac{1}{3}$.

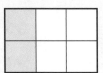

Erica colors $\frac{2}{6}$.

One third is equal to two sixths.

$$\frac{1}{3} = \frac{2}{6}$$

The girls color the same amount of their art papers.

Use the number line to complete the equivalent fractions in problems 1–3.

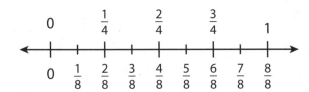

1 $\frac{1}{4} = \frac{\square}{8}$

2 $\frac{6}{8} = \frac{\square}{4}$

3 $\frac{2}{4} = \frac{\square}{\square}$

> ## Vocabulary
>
> **equivalent fractions**
> fractions that name the same point on a number line. $\frac{1}{2}$ and $\frac{2}{4}$ are equivalent.

Shade the models to show equivalent fractions in problems 4 and 5. Then fill in the blanks to write equivalent fractions.

 4

$$\frac{1}{2} \quad = \quad \frac{\square}{8}$$

 5

$$\frac{2}{3} \quad = \quad \frac{\square}{6}$$

Draw lines and shade to show equivalent fractions in problems 6 and 7. Then fill in the blanks to write equivalent fractions.

 6

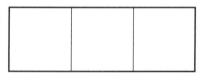

$$\frac{1}{2} \quad = \quad \frac{\square}{4}$$

7

$$\frac{4}{6} \quad = \quad \frac{\square}{3}$$

8   What is a fraction equivalent to $\frac{4}{4}$? Explain how you know.

Develop Writing a Whole Number as a Fraction

Read and try to solve the problem below.

> Kacey uses 2 boards of the same size to build a birdhouse. He cuts each board into fourths. How can you write the number 2 as a fraction to find how many fourths Kacey cuts the boards into?

TRY IT

 Math Toolkit

- fraction tiles
- fraction circles
- fraction bars
- fraction models
- number lines
- grid paper

DISCUSS IT

Ask your partner: How did you get started?

Tell your partner: A model I used was . . . It helped me . . .

Explore different ways to understand writing a whole number as a fraction.

> **Kacey uses 2 boards of the same size to build a birdhouse. He cuts each board into fourths. How can you write the number 2 as a fraction to find how many fourths Kacey cuts the boards into?**

PICTURE IT

You can use models to help you write a whole number as a fraction.

The fraction bars below show 2 wholes, each divided into fourths.

Each part is $\frac{1}{4}$ of a whole. There are eight $\frac{1}{4}$s in all.

MODEL IT

You can use a number line to help you write a whole number as a fraction.

This number line shows whole numbers on the top and fourths on the bottom.

0				1				2
0	$\frac{1}{4}$	$\frac{2}{4}$	$\frac{3}{4}$	$\frac{4}{4}$	$\frac{5}{4}$	$\frac{6}{4}$	$\frac{7}{4}$	$\frac{8}{4}$

Notice that each whole number has an equivalent fraction with a denominator of 4.

CONNECT IT

Now you will use the problem from the previous page to help you understand how to write a whole number as a fraction.

1 Look at the models in **Picture It**. How many equal parts are shown in 1 whole?

Explain how you know.

2 How many equal parts are shown in 2 wholes? Explain how you know.

3 Complete the sentences to show the fraction that is equivalent to 2.

Use words: Two wholes equals ....

Use a fraction: 2 = ...

How many fourths does Kacey cut the boards into?

4 Explain how to find a fraction equivalent to a whole number.

5 REFLECT

Look back at your **Try It**, strategies by classmates, and **Picture It** and **Model It**. Which models or strategies do you like best for writing a whole number as a fraction? Explain.

....

....

....

....

APPLY IT

Use what you just learned to solve these problems.

6 Use the model below to write a fraction equivalent to 3.

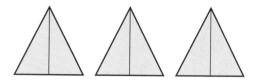

Solution ....

7 Louisa has 2 ribbons that are the same length. She cuts each one into eighths. Use the number line below to help you write the number 2 as a fraction to show how many eighths she cuts the ribbons into.

Solution ....

8 Draw a model to show $3 = \frac{18}{6}$. Show your work.

Practice Writing a Whole Number as a Fraction

Study the Example showing different ways to write whole numbers as fractions. Then solve problems 1–13.

EXAMPLE

Mrs. Clark cuts 2 same-sized pieces of colored paper into sixths to make strips for paper chains. How many strips does she make?

| $\frac{1}{6}$ | $\frac{1}{6}$ | $\frac{1}{6}$ | $\frac{1}{6}$ | $\frac{1}{6}$ | $\frac{1}{6}$ |

| $\frac{1}{6}$ | $\frac{1}{6}$ | $\frac{1}{6}$ | $\frac{1}{6}$ | $\frac{1}{6}$ | $\frac{1}{6}$ |

1 whole = six $\frac{1}{6}$s

$$1 = \frac{6}{6}$$

2 wholes = twelve $\frac{1}{6}$s

$$2 = \frac{12}{6}$$

Each strip is $\frac{1}{6}$ of a whole piece of paper.

Mrs. Clark makes 12 strips.

Write the whole numbers as fractions in problems 1–4.

| $\frac{1}{3}$ | $\frac{1}{3}$ | $\frac{1}{3}$ | | $\frac{1}{3}$ | $\frac{1}{3}$ | $\frac{1}{3}$ | | $\frac{1}{3}$ | $\frac{1}{3}$ | $\frac{1}{3}$ |

1 $1 = \dfrac{\square}{3}$

2 $2 = \dfrac{\square}{3}$

3 $3 = \dfrac{\square}{3}$

4 $4 = \dfrac{\square}{3}$

Use this number line to solve problems 5–8.

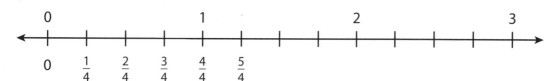

5 $1 = \dfrac{\square}{4}$

6 $2 = \dfrac{\square}{4}$

7 $3 = \dfrac{\square}{4}$

8 $0 = \dfrac{\square}{4}$

Use this number line to solve problems 9–11.

9 One whole is equal to .... eighths.

10 16 eighths is equal to .... wholes.

11 $3 = \dfrac{\square}{8}$

12 Use the model below to write a fraction equivalent to 3.

$3 =$ ....

13 Draw a model to show $2 = \dfrac{8}{4}$.

©Curriculum Associates, LLC Copying is not permitted.

Develop Writing a Whole Number as a Fraction with a Denominator of 1

Read and try to solve the problem below.

> Justin picks 4 green peppers from his garden. He does not cut them into pieces. How can you write the number of peppers Justin picks, 4, as a fraction?

TRY IT

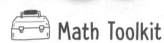 **Math Toolkit**
- fraction circles
- fraction tiles
- fraction bars
- fraction models
- number lines
- grid paper

DISCUSS IT

Ask your partner: Do you agree with me? Why or why not?

Tell your partner: I agree with you about . . . because . . .

Explore different ways to understand writing a whole number as a fraction with a denominator of 1.

> **Justin picks 4 green peppers from his garden. He does not cut them into pieces. How can you write the number of peppers Justin picks, 4, as a fraction?**

PICTURE IT

You can use models to help you write a whole number as a fraction with a denominator of 1.

Each circle stands for 1 green pepper.

They are not divided into pieces, so each whole has one part.

MODEL IT

You can use a number line to help you write a whole number as a fraction with a denominator of 1.

This number line shows whole numbers on the top and fractions on the bottom.

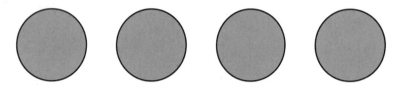

Notice that each whole number has an equivalent fraction. The spaces between whole numbers are not divided into parts. Each whole number has one part, so the denominator of each equivalent fraction is 1.

CONNECT IT

Now you will use the problem from the previous page to help you understand how to write a whole number as a fraction with a denominator of 1.

1 Look at the models in **Picture It**. Explain how you know each whole has only 1 part.

2 How many parts do the 4 green peppers make? ....

3 What does the numerator of a fraction show?

4 What does the denominator of a fraction show?

5 Write a fraction equivalent to 4. Use the fraction below to help you.

$$\frac{\text{number of parts described}}{\text{number of equal parts in the whole}}$$ ....

6 Explain how to write a whole number as a fraction with a denominator of 1.

7 REFLECT

Look back at your **Try It**, strategies by classmates, and **Picture It** and **Model It**. Which models or strategies do you like best for writing a whole number as a fraction with a denominator of 1? Explain.

....

....

....

....

APPLY IT

Use what you just learned to solve these problems.

8 Use the model below to write a fraction equivalent to 6.

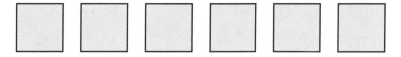

Solution ....

9 Draw a model to show $\frac{5}{1} = 5$.

10 Oscar has 3 loaves of bread that he has not sliced yet. Use a number line to write the pieces of bread Oscar has as a fraction. Show your work.

Solution ....

Practice Writing a Whole Number as a Fraction with a Denominator of 1

Study the Example showing how to write a whole number as a fraction with a denominator of 1. Then solve problems 1–14.

EXAMPLE

The spaces between whole numbers on this number line are not divided into smaller parts. So, each whole has only 1 part.

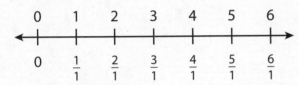

The number line shows that $\frac{3}{1}$ is equal to 3.

$\frac{3}{1}$ is a fraction name for 3.

Write the whole number for each fraction in problems 1–4.

1 $\frac{4}{1}$ = ...

2 $\frac{2}{1}$ = ...

3 $\frac{5}{1}$ = ...

4 $\frac{8}{1}$ = ...

Write a fraction with a denominator of 1 for each whole number in problems 5–8.

5 2 = ...

6 5 = ...

7 1 = ...

8 7 = ...

Write the whole number for each fraction in problems 9 and 10.

9 $\dfrac{9}{1} =$ ....

10 $\dfrac{10}{1} =$ ....

Write a fraction with a denominator of 1 for each whole number in problems 11 and 12.

11 $12 =$ ....

12 $18 =$ ....

13 Explain how to write a whole number as a fraction with a denominator of 1.

14 Bella says this model shows 3 wholes. She says it shows that if you write the whole number 3 as a fraction, you have to write $3 = \dfrac{12}{4}$.
How can you explain to Bella that there are other ways to write 3 as a fraction?

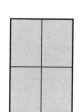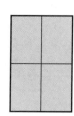

> ## Vocabulary
>
> **numerator** the number above the line in a fraction; it tells how many equal parts are being described.
>
> **denominator** the number below the line in a fraction; it tells how many equal parts are in the whole.

Refine Finding Equivalent Fractions

Complete the Example below. Then solve problems 1–9.

EXAMPLE

Caleb and Hannah buy two melons that are the same size. Caleb cuts his melon into fourths. Hannah cuts her melon into eighths. Hannah eats $\frac{4}{8}$ of her melon. Caleb eats an equal amount of his melon. What fraction of his melon does Caleb eat?

Look at how you could show your work using a model.

Solution ....

The student used solid lines to show fourths. She used dashed lines to show how to divide fourths to make eighths.

PAIR/SHARE
How could you solve this problem using a number line?

APPLY IT

1 Matt says $\frac{3}{3}$ is equivalent to 1. Elisa says $\frac{8}{8}$ is equivalent to 1. Who is correct? Show your work.

How many thirds are in 1 whole? How many eighths are in 1 whole?

PAIR/SHARE
What is another fraction that is equivalent to 1?

Solution ....

2 Write two fractions that are equivalent to 5. Show your work.

There will be 5 wholes in all. Think about how many parts will be in each whole.

Solution ....

PAIR/SHARE
How did you decide what denominators to use in your fractions?

3 Kaia ate $\frac{3}{6}$ of a banana. Zoie ate an equivalent amount. Which fraction shows how much of a banana Zoie ate?

Ⓐ $\frac{1}{3}$

Ⓑ $\frac{2}{3}$

Ⓒ $\frac{5}{8}$

Ⓓ $\frac{1}{2}$

Landon chose Ⓐ as the correct answer. How did he get that answer?

Find $\frac{3}{6}$ on a number line. What is another fraction that names the same location?

PAIR/SHARE
Does Landon's answer make sense?

4 Which model shows a fraction equivalent to $\frac{2}{6}$?

     Ⓐ   Ⓑ   Ⓒ   Ⓓ

5 Draw a model to find a fraction equivalent to $\frac{1}{4}$. Show your work.

$\frac{1}{4}$ is equivalent to ....

6 Look at point *P* on the number line.

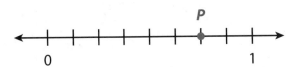

Does the point on each number line below represent a fraction equivalent to the fraction shown by point *P*?

	Yes	No
(number line, point at 3/4)	Ⓐ	Ⓑ
(number line, point at 1/2)	Ⓒ	Ⓓ
(number line, point at 1/2)	Ⓔ	Ⓕ

7 Does the point on each number line represent one whole?

	Yes	No
0 $\frac{1}{1}$ $\frac{2}{1}$ $\frac{3}{1}$ $\frac{4}{1}$	Ⓐ	Ⓑ
0 $\frac{1}{1}$ $\frac{2}{1}$ $\frac{3}{1}$ $\frac{4}{1}$	Ⓒ	Ⓓ
0 $\frac{1}{4}$ $\frac{2}{4}$ $\frac{3}{4}$ 1	Ⓔ	Ⓕ
0 $\frac{1}{4}$ $\frac{2}{4}$ $\frac{3}{4}$ $\frac{4}{4}$	Ⓖ	Ⓗ

8 Use the number line to find a fraction equivalent to 3. Show your work.

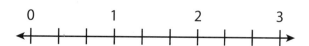

3 is equivalent to ....

9 MATH JOURNAL

Write two fractions equivalent to 4 using the denominators 1 and 3. Use a number line to show how you found your answers.

✓ SELF CHECK Go back to the Unit 4 Opener and see what you can check off.

Understand Comparing Fractions

Dear Family,

This week your child is exploring comparing fractions.

When two fractions have the same denominator, the numerator tells you which is more and which is less.

These fractions are built from the unit fraction $\frac{1}{6}$. So, the fraction with the most parts in the numerator is more.

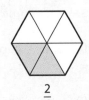

$\frac{2}{6}$ $\frac{4}{6}$

$\frac{4}{6}$ is more than $\frac{2}{6}$ because 4 parts is more than 2 parts when all the parts are equal in size.

If two fractions have the same numerator, then the denominator can tell you which fraction is greater.

Compare the denominators of $\frac{1}{3}$ and $\frac{1}{8}$. When something is cut into 3 equal pieces, the pieces are larger than if the object is cut into 8 equal pieces. When there are fewer parts, each part is larger. So, $\frac{1}{3}$ is greater than $\frac{1}{8}$.

This also shows that $\frac{2}{3}$ is greater than $\frac{2}{8}$, since 2 large pieces is more than 2 small pieces.

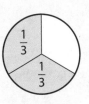 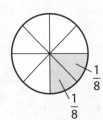

Invite your child to share what he or she knows about comparing fractions by doing the following activity together.

ACTIVITY COMPARING FRACTIONS

Do this activity with your child to understand comparing fractions.

Materials 2 small identical glasses or jars; measuring cups for $\frac{1}{4}$-, $\frac{1}{3}$-, and $\frac{1}{2}$-cup, colored water

Use measured amounts of water to compare fractions. First experiment with fractions that have the same denominator by using only the $\frac{1}{4}$-cup measure.

- Work with your child to pour $\frac{2}{4}$ cup of colored water into one glass (call it Glass *A*) and $\frac{3}{4}$ cup into the other glass (call it Glass *B*). Place them side by side and compare. Which is more, $\frac{2}{4}$ or $\frac{3}{4}$?

- Repeat to compare $\frac{2}{4}$ and $\frac{4}{4}$, $\frac{3}{4}$ and $\frac{4}{4}$, $\frac{2}{4}$ and $\frac{6}{4}$. Talk about how you can predict which will be more even before you measure the water into the glasses.

Now experiment with fractions that have different denominators but have the same numerator.

- Work with your child to pour $\frac{1}{3}$ cup of colored water into one glass (call it Glass *A*) and $\frac{1}{4}$ cup into the other glass (call this Glass *B*). Place them side by side and compare. Which is more, $\frac{1}{3}$ or $\frac{1}{4}$?

- Empty the glasses. Pour $\frac{2}{3}$ cup of water into Glass *A* and $\frac{2}{4}$ cup into Glass *B*. Which is more, $\frac{2}{3}$ or $\frac{2}{4}$? Then compare $\frac{3}{3}$ and $\frac{3}{4}$.

- What pattern do you notice? How can you use that pattern to predict which is more, $\frac{7}{3}$ or $\frac{7}{4}$?

- Continue to experiment with other measurements. For example, use the measuring cups to compare $\frac{3}{2}$ to $\frac{3}{4}$ or to compare $\frac{3}{2}$ to $\frac{1}{2}$. Have fun!

Glass *A*   **Glass *B***

Explore Comparing Fractions

How do you compare fractions?

Learning Target
- Compare two fractions with the same numerator or the same denominator by reasoning about their size. Recognize that comparisons are valid only when the two fractions refer to the same whole. Record the results of comparisons with the symbols >, =, or <, and justify the conclusions, e.g., by using a visual fraction model.

SMP 1, 2, 3, 4, 5, 6, 7

MODEL IT
Complete the problems below.

1 **a.** Shade the models at the right to show the fractions $\frac{1}{4}$ and $\frac{2}{4}$.

b. Use the fractions $\frac{1}{4}$ and $\frac{2}{4}$ to complete the sentence.

.... is greater than ....

2 Use the number line at the right to compare $\frac{1}{4}$ and $\frac{2}{4}$.

a. Which fraction is greater? ....

b. When comparing two fractions with the same denominator, how can the numerators tell you which fraction is greater? Explain.

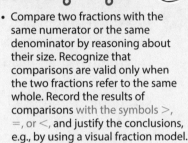

$\frac{1}{4}$ shaded $\frac{2}{4}$ shaded

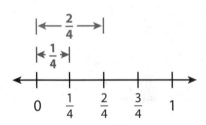

3 Compare the shaded parts of the models below. Can you use these models to show that the sentence in problem 1b is true? Explain.

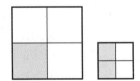

DISCUSS IT
- Did you and your partner explain the answer to problem 2b in the same way?

- I think the wholes have to be the same size when comparing fractions because . . .

MODEL IT

Complete the problems below.

 a. Which model at the right has more parts? ....

b. Which model has smaller parts? ....

c. Shade $\frac{1}{3}$ of model A and $\frac{1}{8}$ of model B.

d. Use the fractions $\frac{1}{3}$ and $\frac{1}{8}$ to complete the sentence.

.... is greater than ....

A   B

 a. Label each part of each model at the right
with the unit fraction it represents.

b. Shade 3 parts of each model. What
fraction does each model show?

C: .... D: ....

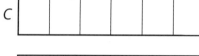

C

D

c. Which unit fraction from Part a is greater? ....

d. Which fraction from Part b is greater? ....

e. When comparing two fractions with the same numerator,
how can the denominators tell you which fraction is greater?
Explain.

DISCUSS IT

• Did you and your partner
explain the answer to
problem 5e in the same
way?

• I think that the lesser unit
fraction has the greater
denominator because . . .

6 REFLECT

Explain how you can compare unit fractions such as $\frac{1}{3}$ and $\frac{1}{8}$.

....

....

....

Prepare for Comparing Fractions

1 Think about what you know about fractions. Fill in each box. Use words, numbers, and pictures. Show as many ideas as you can.

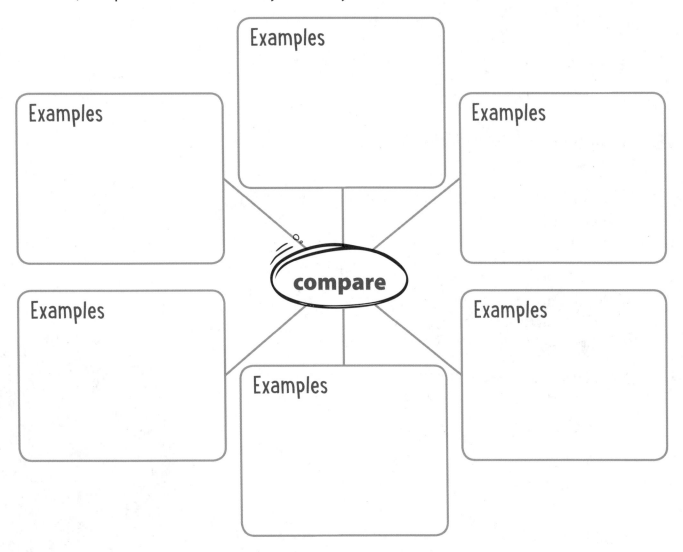

2 Shade the models to show the fractions $\frac{2}{6}$ and $\frac{4}{6}$. Then complete the sentence to compare the fractions.

.... is less than ....

$\frac{2}{6}$ shaded $\frac{4}{6}$ shaded

Solve.

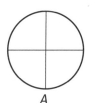

3 a. Which model at the right has fewer parts? ....

b. Which model has larger parts? ....

c. Shade $\frac{1}{4}$ of model A and $\frac{1}{6}$ of model B.

d. Use the fractions $\frac{1}{4}$ and $\frac{1}{6}$ to complete the sentence.

.... is less than ....

4 a. Label each part of each model at the right with the unit fraction it represents.

b. Shade 2 parts of each model. What fraction does each model show?

C: .... D: ....

c. Which unit fraction from Part a is less? ....

d. Which fraction from Part b is less? ....

e. When comparing two fractions with the same numerator, how can the denominators tell you which fraction is less? Explain.

Develop Understanding of Comparing Fractions

MODEL IT: AREA MODELS

Try these problems.

1 Write the fraction shaded below each model. Circle the fraction that is greater.

a.   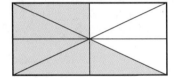   **b.**

....

2 Write the fraction shaded below the first model. Shade the second model to show a greater fraction. Write the greater fraction.

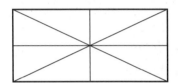

....

3 Write the fraction shaded below the first model. Divide and shade the second model to show a fraction that is less than the first fraction but has the same numerator. Write the lesser fraction.

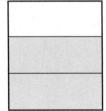   

....

DISCUSS IT

• How do you know the model you divided and shaded in problem 3 shows a lesser fraction?

• I think area models are a good way to compare fractions because . . .

MODEL IT: NUMBER LINES

Use the number lines to compare fractions.

4 Look at the fractions on the number lines. Circle the fraction that is less.

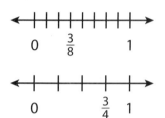

5 Look at the fractions on the number lines. Circle the fraction that is greater.

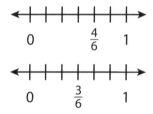

CONNECT IT

Complete the problems below.

6 How is comparing fractions with area models like comparing fractions with number lines? How is it different?

DISCUSS IT

• Did you and your partner choose the same fractions for problems 4 and 5?

• I think number lines can be used to compare fractions because . . .

7 Which is less, $\frac{5}{8}$ or $\frac{5}{6}$? How do you know?

Practice Comparing Fractions

Study how the Example uses models to compare fractions.
Then solve problems 1–8.

EXAMPLE

The two rectangles are the same size.

If you make 8 equal parts, the parts are smaller than if you make 4 equal parts.

$\frac{1}{8}$ is less than $\frac{1}{4}$.

$\frac{1}{4}$ is greater than $\frac{1}{8}$.

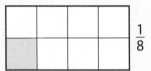

Write the fraction for the shaded parts in problems 1–3.
Circle the fraction that is *greater*.

1

Fractions: ....

2

Fractions: ....

3

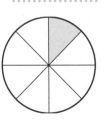

Fractions: ....

Write the fraction for the shaded parts in problems 4 and 5.
Circle the fraction that is *less*.

4

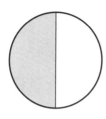

Fractions: ....

5

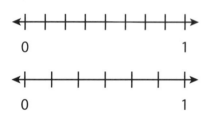

Fractions: ....

6 Label the fractions $\frac{4}{8}$ and $\frac{4}{6}$ on the number lines.

Then circle the fraction that is *greater*.

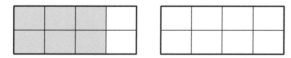

7 Write the fraction for the shaded rectangle. Then shade the second
rectangle to show a fraction that is less. Write the fraction.

Fractions: ....

8 Write a fraction less than $\frac{1}{4}$ that has a numerator of 1.

Refine Ideas About Comparing Fractions

APPLY IT

Complete these problems on your own.

1 CREATE

Draw an area model or number line to show $\frac{5}{8}$. Explain how to find a lesser fraction with the same denominator and give an example.

2 JUSTIFY

Jace and Lianna each bake a loaf of bread. Jace cuts his loaf into halves, and Lianna cuts her loaf into thirds as shown. Jace says their loaves show that $\frac{1}{2}$ is less than $\frac{1}{3}$. Lianna says they do not. Who is correct? Explain.

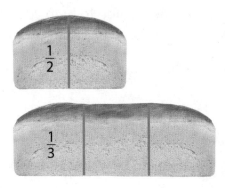

3 EXPLAIN

Mario paints $\frac{2}{6}$ of a wall in his bedroom. Mei Lyn paints $\frac{2}{4}$ of a wall in her bedroom. The two walls are the same size. Explain how you know who paints more of their wall.

PAIR/SHARE

Discuss your solutions for these three problems with a partner.

Use what you have learned to complete problem 4.

4 Mrs. Ericson makes sandwiches for her 4 children. Each sandwich is the same size. After lunch, each child has a different fraction of sandwich left. Matt has $\frac{1}{4}$ left, Elisa has $\frac{3}{8}$ left, Carl has $\frac{3}{4}$ left, and Riley has $\frac{7}{8}$ left.

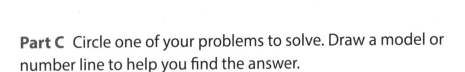

Part A Use the information above to write a word problem about comparing two fractions with the same numerator.

Part B Use the information above to write a word problem about comparing two fractions with the same denominator.

Part C Circle one of your problems to solve. Draw a model or number line to help you find the answer.

Explain how you could use unit fractions to solve your problem.

5 MATH JOURNAL

Choose two fractions to compare. Draw models to help you explain how you know which fraction is greater.

Use Symbols to Compare Fractions

Dear Family,

This week your child is learning about using symbols to compare fractions.

To compare fractions, you can use the symbols $<$, $>$, or $=$.

$<$ means *less than*. $>$ means *greater than*.

Which symbol would you use to compare $\frac{4}{8}$ and $\frac{4}{6}$?

It can help to use area models to compare fractions. Both fractions must be represented using same-sized wholes.

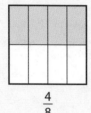

$\frac{4}{8}$

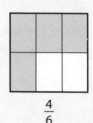

$\frac{4}{6}$

You can also use number lines to compare fractions. Again, you must use same-sized wholes.

The top number line is divided into eighths and shows $\frac{4}{8}$.

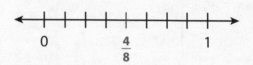

0          $\frac{4}{8}$ 1

The bottom number line is divided into sixths and shows $\frac{4}{6}$.

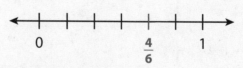

0          $\frac{4}{6}$ 1

Both methods show that $\frac{4}{8}$ is less than $\frac{4}{6}$. This also means that $\frac{4}{6}$ is greater than $\frac{4}{8}$. Using symbols, you can write the comparison two different ways.

$$\frac{4}{8} < \frac{4}{6} \quad \text{and} \quad \frac{4}{6} > \frac{4}{8}$$

Invite your child to share what he or she knows about using symbols to compare fractions by doing the following activity together.

ACTIVITY COMPARING FRACTIONS WITH SYMBOLS

Do this activity with your child to practice using symbols to compare fractions.

Materials number cards below, scissors, 2 bags, recording sheet below

Give your child practice comparing fractions with this activity.

- Cut out the cards below. Put the number cards in one bag and the Numerator and Denominator cards in the other bag. Players take turns.

- Player 1 draws a number from one bag and a Numerator or Denominator card from the other bag.

- Both players write a fraction based on the information. For example, if the 4 and Numerator cards are drawn, both players make up a fraction with 4 as the numerator. Write the fractions in the same row of the table below.

- Discuss with your child and then record the correct symbol in the table to compare the fractions. Remember: < means *less than* and > means *greater than*.

- Return both cards to the bags and draw two more. Play a total of five rounds.

Player 1 Fraction	< or > or =	Player 2 Fraction

1	2	3	4	6	8

Numerator	Denominator

Explore Using Symbols to Compare Fractions

Previously you learned how to compare fractions. In this lesson you will use the symbols $<$, $>$, and $=$ to show how fractions compare. Use what you know to try to solve the problem below.

> Erica and Ethan have same-sized glasses. Erica's glass is $\frac{4}{6}$ full of juice. Ethan's glass is $\frac{5}{6}$ full of juice. Compare $\frac{4}{6}$ and $\frac{5}{6}$ using $<$, $>$, or $=$. Who has more juice?

Learning Target

- Compare two fractions with the same numerator or the same denominator by reasoning about their size. Recognize that comparisons are valid only when the two fractions refer to the same whole. Record the results of comparisons with the symbols $>$, $=$, or $<$, and justify the conclusions, e.g., by using a visual fraction model.

SMP 1, 2, 3, 4, 5, 6, 7

TRY IT

 Math Toolkit

- fraction tiles
- fraction bars
- fraction models
- number lines
- grid paper
- sticky notes

DISCUSS IT

Ask your partner: How did you get started?

Tell your partner: I started by . . .

CONNECT IT

① LOOK BACK

Who has more juice? How did you compare $\frac{4}{6}$ and $\frac{5}{6}$ to find out?

② LOOK AHEAD

You can use the symbols $<$, $>$, or $=$ to compare fractions just as you did to compare whole numbers. Remember that the symbol opens to the greater fraction and points to the lesser fraction.

greater fraction $>$ lesser fraction   and   lesser fraction $<$ greater fraction

You can use words or a symbol to compare fractions.

$<$ means *less than*. $>$ means *greater than*. $=$ means *equal to*.

a. Use words and a symbol to compare $\frac{1}{2}$ and $\frac{1}{3}$.

$\frac{1}{2}$ is .... $\frac{1}{3}$. $\frac{1}{2}$ ◯ $\frac{1}{3}$
    words   **symbol**

b. Use words and a symbol to compare $\frac{1}{4}$ and $\frac{1}{2}$.

$\frac{1}{4}$ is .... $\frac{1}{2}$. $\frac{1}{4}$ ◯ $\frac{1}{2}$
    words   **symbol**

c. Use words and a symbol to compare $\frac{1}{2}$ and $\frac{1}{2}$.

$\frac{1}{2}$ is .... $\frac{1}{2}$. $\frac{1}{2}$ ◯ $\frac{1}{2}$
    words   **symbol**

③ REFLECT

What helps you remember what the symbols $>$ and $<$ mean when comparing two numbers?

....

....

Prepare for Using Symbols to Compare Fractions

1 Think about what you know about fractions. Fill in each box. Use words, numbers, and pictures. Show as many ideas as you can.

Word	In My Own Words	Example
greater than		
less than		
equal to		
>		
<		
=		

2 Use words and a symbol to compare $\frac{1}{4}$ and $\frac{1}{3}$.

$\frac{1}{4}$ is .... $\frac{1}{3}$.
words

$\frac{1}{4}$ ◯ $\frac{1}{3}$
symbol

$\frac{1}{4}$ $\frac{1}{3}$

3 Solve the problem. Show your work.

Kim and Armen each buy same-sized sandwiches.

Kim ate $\frac{6}{8}$ of her sandwich. Armen ate $\frac{5}{8}$ of his sandwich.

Compare $\frac{6}{8}$ and $\frac{5}{8}$ using <, >, or =. Who ate more?

Solution ....

4 Check your answer. Show your work.

Develop Comparing Fractions Using Symbols

Read and try to solve the problem below.

Compare $\frac{4}{8}$ and $\frac{4}{6}$ using <, >, or =.

TRY IT

Math Toolkit
- fraction tiles
- fraction bars
- fraction circles
- fraction models
- number lines
- grid paper
- sticky notes

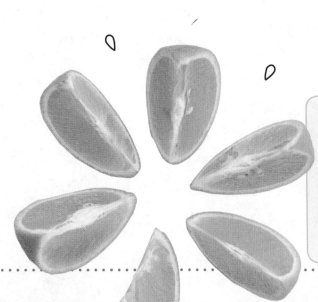

DISCUSS IT

Ask your partner: Why did you choose that strategy?

Tell your partner: The strategy I used to find the answer was . . .

Explore different ways to understand comparing fractions.

> **Compare $\frac{4}{8}$ and $\frac{4}{6}$ using <, >, or =.**

PICTURE IT

You can use area models to help you compare fractions.

The models show same-sized wholes.

This model shows $\frac{4}{8}$.

This model shows $\frac{4}{6}$.

MODEL IT

You can also use number lines to help you compare fractions.

The number lines also show same-sized wholes.

This number line shows $\frac{4}{8}$.

This number line is divided into eighths.

This number line shows $\frac{4}{6}$.

This number line is divided into sixths.

CONNECT IT

Now you will use the problem from the previous page to help you understand how to compare fractions using symbols.

1 Look at the models in **Picture It**. How can you use them to compare $\frac{4}{8}$ and $\frac{4}{6}$?

2 Look at the number lines in **Model It**. How can you use them to compare the two fractions?

3 Compare with words: 4 eighths is .... than 4 sixths.

Compare with a symbol: $\frac{4}{8}$ ◯ $\frac{4}{6}$?

4 Now switch the order of the fractions.

Compare with words: 4 sixths is .... than 4 eighths.

Compare with a symbol: $\frac{4}{6}$ ◯ $\frac{4}{8}$?

5 Explain how to use symbols to compare two fractions.

6 **REFLECT**

Look back at your **Try It**, strategies by classmates, and **Picture It** and **Model It**. Which models or strategies do you like best for using symbols to compare fractions? Explain.

....

....

....

....

....

Lesson 25 Use Symbols to Compare Fractions   **541**

APPLY IT

Use what you just learned to solve these problems.

7 Compare each pair of fractions using <, >, or =. Shade the models to help.

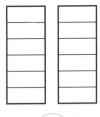

$\dfrac{4}{6}$ ◯ $\dfrac{2}{6}$ $\dfrac{2}{8}$ ◯ $\dfrac{2}{2}$ $\dfrac{1}{2}$ ◯ $\dfrac{1}{2}$

8 Compare each pair of fractions using <, >, or =. Use the number lines to help.

$\dfrac{3}{4}$ ◯ $\dfrac{3}{4}$

$\dfrac{2}{4}$ ◯ $\dfrac{2}{3}$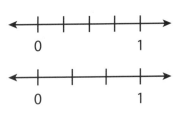

$\dfrac{2}{3}$ ◯ $\dfrac{1}{3}$

9 Manny and Sarah are reading the same book. Manny has read $\dfrac{5}{8}$ of the book. Sarah has read $\dfrac{5}{6}$ of the book. Compare $\dfrac{5}{8}$ and $\dfrac{5}{6}$ using <, >, or =. Who has read more? Show your work.

Solution ....

Practice Comparing Fractions Using Symbols

**Study the Example showing how to use symbols to compare fractions.
Then solve problems 1–16.**

EXAMPLE

Compare the fractions $\frac{3}{6}$ and $\frac{3}{8}$.

$\frac{3}{6}$ is greater than $\frac{3}{8}$.

$\qquad \frac{3}{6} > \frac{3}{8}$

$\frac{3}{8}$ is less than $\frac{3}{6}$.

$\qquad \frac{3}{8} < \frac{3}{6}$

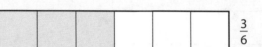

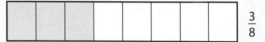

Use the models to compare the fractions in problems 1 and 2. Write <, >, or =.

1

$\frac{3}{8} \bigcirc \frac{6}{8}$

2

$\frac{1}{3} \bigcirc \frac{1}{2}$

Use the number lines to compare the fractions in problems 3–5. Write <, >, or =.

3 $\frac{3}{8} \bigcirc \frac{5}{8}$

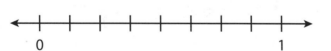

4 $\frac{4}{6} \bigcirc \frac{1}{6}$

5 $\frac{5}{8} \bigcirc \frac{5}{6}$

Write the fraction shown in problems 6–10.

6

7

8

9

10

Compare the fractions in problems 11–14. You can use the models above to help you. Write <, >, or =.

11 $\frac{2}{4}\bigcirc\frac{2}{6}$

$\frac{2}{6}\bigcirc\frac{2}{4}$

12 $\frac{2}{3}\bigcirc\frac{2}{6}$

$\frac{2}{6}\bigcirc\frac{2}{3}$

13 $\frac{3}{4}\bigcirc\frac{3}{8}$

$\frac{3}{8}\bigcirc\frac{3}{4}$

14 $\frac{2}{4}\bigcirc\frac{3}{4}$

$\frac{3}{4}\bigcirc\frac{2}{4}$

Write a fraction to make the statement true in problems 15 and 16.

15 $\frac{6}{8} >$ ....

16 $\frac{1}{4} >$ ....

Refine Using Symbols to Compare Fractions

Complete the Example below. Then solve problems 1–8.

EXAMPLE

Su and Anthony live the same distance from school.
Su bikes $\frac{3}{4}$ of the way to school in five minutes.
Anthony walks $\frac{1}{4}$ of the way to school in five minutes.
Compare the fractions using $<$, $>$, or $=$. Who travels
the greater distance in these five minutes?

Look at how you could show your work using a number line.

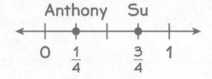

Solution ....

> The fractions have the same denominator, so they are easy to compare on the same number line.

PAIR/SHARE
How do you find the greater number on a number line?

APPLY IT

1. Julia and Mackenzie have the same number of homework
   problems. Julia has done $\frac{1}{3}$ of her homework. Mackenzie has
   done $\frac{1}{2}$ of her homework. Compare the fractions using $<$, $>$,
   or $=$. Which student has done less of her homework?
   Show your work.

> What do you need to think about when you compare fractions that have different denominators?

PAIR/SHARE
How did you know which fraction was less?

Solution ....

2 Deon and Rob each get same-sized packs of crackers. Deon eats $\frac{3}{6}$ of his crackers. Rob eats $\frac{3}{4}$ of his crackers. Compare the fractions using $<$, $>$, or $=$. Who eats more of his crackers? Show your work.

I think drawing a model might help. Be sure the wholes are the same size.

PAIR/SHARE
Which fraction is made of greater unit fractions? How do you know?

Solution . . . .

3 Which fraction goes in the blank to make the comparison true?

$$\frac{5}{8} < \underline{\hspace{1cm}}$$

Ⓐ $\frac{5}{8}$

Ⓑ $\frac{4}{8}$

Ⓒ $\frac{6}{8}$

Ⓓ $\frac{1}{8}$

Blake chose Ⓐ as the correct answer. How did he get that answer?

Is $\frac{5}{8}$ less than or greater than the fraction that goes in the blank?

PAIR/SHARE
Does Blake's answer make sense?

4 Which fraction goes in the blank to make the comparison true?

$$\underline{\qquad} < \frac{2}{8}$$

Ⓐ $\frac{2}{4}$

Ⓑ $\frac{4}{8}$

Ⓒ $\frac{1}{8}$

Ⓓ $\frac{2}{6}$

5 Which model can you use to compare the fractions $\frac{1}{3}$ and $\frac{1}{6}$?

Ⓐ
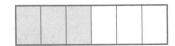

Ⓑ

Ⓒ

Ⓓ

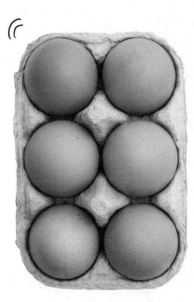

6 Write a number from the list below in each box to make the statement true.

6   8   1   3   4

$$\frac{\boxed{}}{8} < \frac{\boxed{}}{8}$$

7 Look at the comparison below.

$$\underline{\qquad} < \frac{3}{4}$$

Tyrone writes a fraction in the blank to make the comparison true. His fraction has a 3 in the numerator. What fraction could Tyrone have written? Show your work.

Solution ....

8 MATH JOURNAL

Tran and Noah are each given the same amount of clay in art class. Tran divides his clay into 3 equal pieces. He uses 2 pieces to make a bowl. Noah divides his clay into 4 equal pieces. He also uses 2 pieces to make a bowl. Tran says that he has more clay left over than Noah. Is Tran correct? Explain.

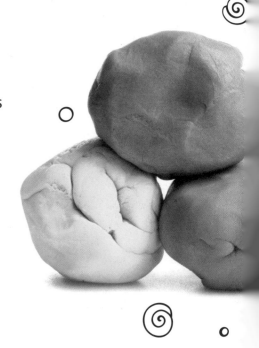

☑ SELF CHECK Go back to the Unit 4 Opener and see what you can check off.

Measure Length and Plot Data on Line Plots

Dear Family,

This week your child is learning to measure length in fractions of an inch and plot the data on line plots.

A line plot is a graph using marks above a number line to show how many objects are in different categories. In this lesson, using categories based on fractional measurements of length gives your child practice using a ruler, reading and writing mixed numbers such as $2\frac{1}{2}$, and locating fractions on a number line.

Here is a table showing the lengths of some dragonfly wings. The wings have been measured to the nearest $\frac{1}{4}$ inch.

Lengths of Dragonfly Wings									
Wing	A	B	C	D	E	F	G	H	I
Length (in.)	$\frac{3}{4}$	$\frac{1}{2}$	$1\frac{1}{4}$	$1\frac{1}{2}$	$1\frac{1}{4}$	$\frac{3}{4}$	1	$1\frac{1}{4}$	1

The data from the table above are shown on the line plot below. There is an X for each wing length recorded. The line plot sorts the data for you and makes it easy to see things such as what wing length is most common.

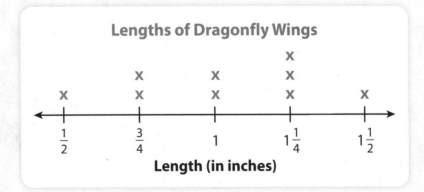

Invite your child to share what he or she knows about measuring length and plotting data on line plots by doing the following activity together.

ACTIVITY MAKING A LINE PLOT

Do this activity with your child to measure length and make a line plot.

Materials 6 different writing tools (pencils, pens, markers, crayons), inch ruler

Work with your child to measure objects and create a line plot to show the data.

• Measure each writing tool to the nearest $\frac{1}{2}$ inch and record in the table below.

Writing Tool Lengths						
Writing tool	A	B	C	D	E	F
Length (to the nearest $\frac{1}{2}$ inch)						

• Now work together to make a line plot.
  • Use the shortest length to label the left end of the number line. Then label the rest of the number line at least up to the longest length.
  • Place one X above the correct mark to show the length of each writing tool.

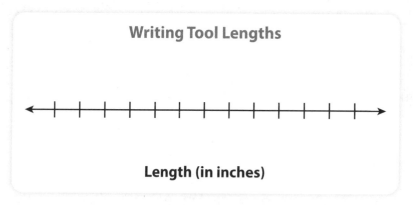

Writing Tool Lengths

Length (in inches)

• Discuss with your child questions such as:
  • *How would the line plot change if you had measured only crayons? Would the Xs likely be closer together or more spread out?*
  • *What if you had measured only pencils?*

You can check your thinking by trying it!

Explore Measuring Length and Plotting Data on Line Plots

Previously you drew picture graphs and bar graphs. In this lesson you will measure objects and draw line plots. Use what you know to try to solve the problem below.

Use a ruler to measure each pencil to the nearest inch. Create a line plot for your data.

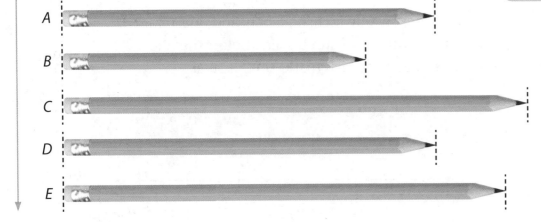

TRY IT

 Math Toolkit

• inch rulers
• number lines
• 1-inch grid paper

 **DISCUSS IT**

Ask your partner: How did you get started?

Tell your partner: I started by . . .

CONNECT IT

1 LOOK BACK

Explain how you found the measurement to the nearest inch for each pencil in order to make your line plot.

2 LOOK AHEAD

You can measure objects to the nearest whole inch, half inch, and quarter inch. Usually fractions are not labeled on a ruler. The number line below the ruler labels the whole-inch, half-inch, and quarter-inch marks on this ruler.

a. You can count by **half inches** on the ruler.

Complete the count by half inches from 0 to 3 inches below.

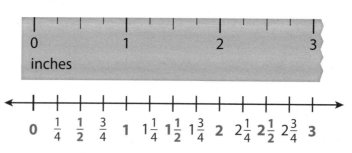

0 inches, $\frac{1}{2}$ inch, 1 inch, ... inches, ... inches, ... inches, ... inches

b. What are the lengths of the red and blue pencils to the nearest half inch?

Red: ....

Blue: ....

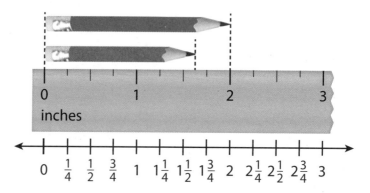

3 REFLECT

Explain how you found the lengths of the pencils to the nearest half inch in problem 2b.

....

....

....

Prepare for Measuring Length and Plotting Data on Line Plots

1 Think about what you know about measurement. Fill in each box. Use words, numbers, and pictures. Show as many ideas as you can.

Word	In My Own Words	Example
nearest inch		
nearest $\frac{1}{2}$ inch		
nearest $\frac{1}{4}$ inch		

2 What is the length of the crayon measured to the nearest inch, nearest $\frac{1}{2}$ inch, and nearest $\frac{1}{4}$ inch?

Nearest inch: .... inches

Nearest $\frac{1}{2}$ inch: .... inches

Nearest $\frac{1}{4}$ inch: .... inches

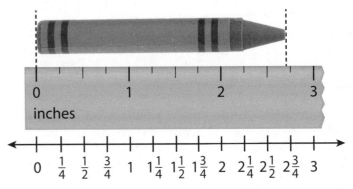

③ Solve the problem. Show your work.

Use a ruler to measure each fish to the nearest inch. Create a line plot for your data.

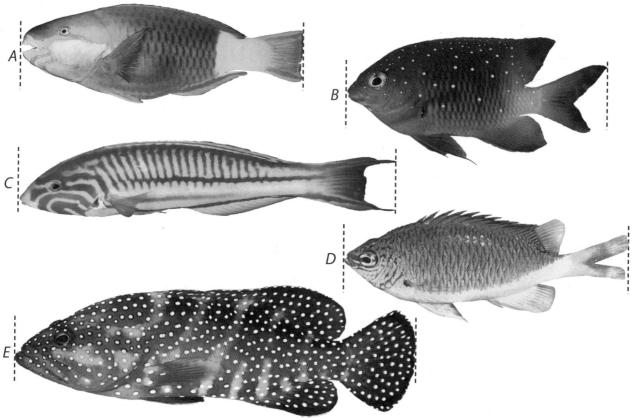

④ Check your answer. Show your work.

Develop Measuring Length

Read and try to solve the problem below.

> Brian is measuring the lengths of 6 earthworms. The earthworms he collected are shown. Describe how he could find the length of each earthworm to the nearest $\frac{1}{4}$ inch.

A
B
C
D
E
F

TRY IT

 **Math Toolkit**
- inch rulers
- number lines
- 1-inch grid paper

DISCUSS IT

Ask your partner: How did you get started?

Tell your partner: I started by . . .

Explore different ways to understand measuring length.

> **Brian is measuring the lengths of 6 earthworms. The earthworms he collected are shown. Describe how he could find the length of each earthworm to the nearest $\frac{1}{4}$ inch.**

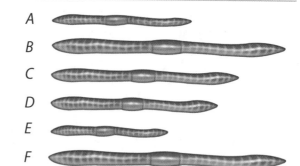

MODEL IT

You can look at an inch ruler to help you understand one-fourth-inch marks.

This ruler shows one-fourth-inch marks.

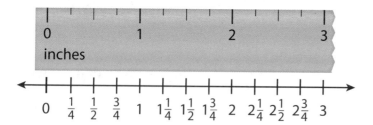

PICTURE IT

You can use an inch ruler to help you understand how to measure length to the nearest $\frac{1}{4}$ inch.

You can measure to the nearest $\frac{1}{4}$ inch.

Line up the **left end** of each earthworm with **0** on the ruler.
Find the **mark** on the ruler that is **closest to the other end** of the earthworm.

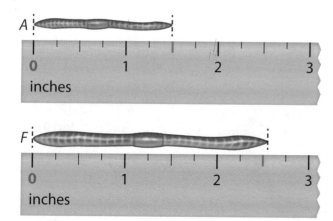

CONNECT IT

Now you will use the problem from the previous page to help you understand how to measure length.

1 Complete the sentence to describe how you begin to measure earthworm *A*.

I line up the left end of the earthworm with .... on the ruler.

2 Look at **Picture It**. Is earthworm *A* longer than or shorter than 1 inch? ....

3 The mark on the ruler that is closest to the other end of earthworm *A* represents

.... inches.

4 Earthworm *A* is .... inches long. Write this length in the table below.

5 Use a ruler to measure earthworms *B*, *C*, *D*, *E*, and *F* to the nearest $\frac{1}{4}$ inch. Write your measurements in the table.

Earthworm Lengths						
Earthworm	*A*	*B*	*C*	*D*	*E*	*F*
Length (in inches)						

6 Explain how you found the length of earthworm *F*.

7 REFLECT

Look back at your **Try It**, strategies by classmates, and **Model It** and **Picture It**. Which models or strategies do you like best for measuring length? Explain.

....

....

....

....

APPLY IT

Use what you just learned to solve these problems.

8 Brian finds two more worms. He labels them *G* and *H*. What are the lengths of the worms to the nearest $\frac{1}{4}$ inch? Show your work.

G   H

Worm *G* is .... inches long.   Worm *H* is .... inches long.

9 Use a ruler to draw a line that is $4\frac{1}{4}$ inches long.

10 Which lines are 3 inches long when measured to the nearest $\frac{1}{2}$ inch?

Ⓐ ────────────────────────

Ⓑ ──────────────────────

Ⓒ ────────────────

Ⓓ ────────────────────────

Ⓔ ──────────────────

Practice Measuring Length

Study the Example showing how to measure length. Then solve problems 1–8.

EXAMPLE

What is the length of the longest crayon?

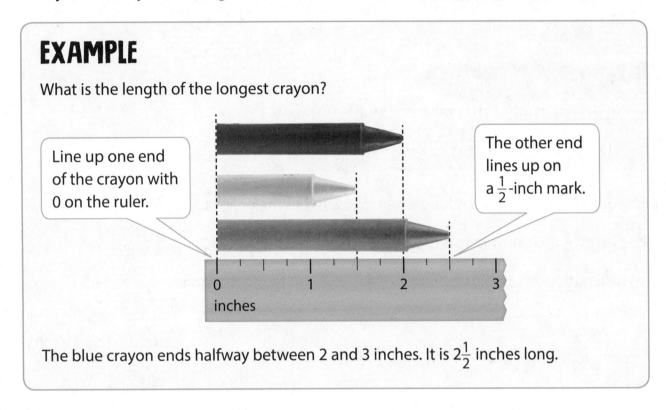

Line up one end of the crayon with 0 on the ruler.

The other end lines up on a $\frac{1}{2}$-inch mark.

The blue crayon ends halfway between 2 and 3 inches. It is $2\frac{1}{2}$ inches long.

1. The tip of the yellow crayon above is between which two inches on the ruler?

   To the nearest $\frac{1}{2}$ inch, how long is the yellow crayon?

2. What is the length of the red crayon above? Tell how you know.

3. To the nearest $\frac{1}{2}$ inch, how long is this green crayon?

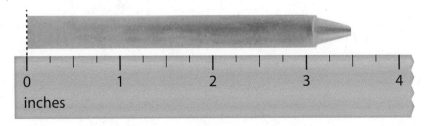

Use the picture below to solve problems 4–6.

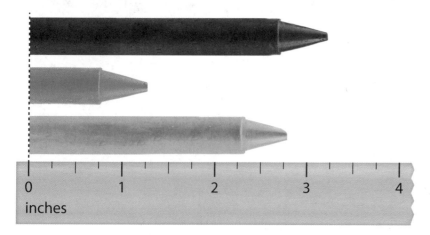

4 Which color crayon is $3\frac{1}{4}$ inches long when measured to the nearest $\frac{1}{4}$ inch?

5 To the nearest $\frac{1}{4}$ inch, how long is the green crayon?

6 Write the length of the orange crayon. Explain how you found the length.

Use the picture below to solve problems 7 and 8.

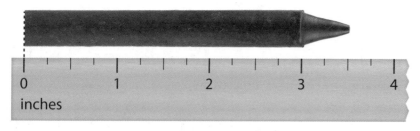

7 To the nearest $\frac{1}{2}$ inch, what is the length of the brown crayon?

8 Can you also measure the brown crayon to the nearest $\frac{1}{4}$ inch? Explain.

Develop Displaying Data in a Line Plot

Read and try to solve the problem below.

> **Brian records the lengths of his earthworms in the table below. Draw a line plot using Brian's measurement data.**

Earthworm Lengths								
Earthworm	A	B	C	D	E	F	G	H
Length (in inches)	$1\frac{1}{2}$	$2\frac{1}{2}$	2	$1\frac{3}{4}$	$1\frac{1}{4}$	$2\frac{1}{2}$	$1\frac{1}{2}$	$2\frac{3}{4}$

TRY IT

Math Toolkit
- inch rulers
- number lines
- 1-inch grid paper

DISCUSS IT

Ask your partner: How did you get started?

Tell your partner: I started by . . .

Explore different ways to understand how to display data.

> **Brian records the lengths of his earthworms in the table below. Draw a line plot using Brian's measurement data.**

Earthworm Lengths								
Earthworm	*A*	*B*	*C*	*D*	*E*	*F*	*G*	*H*
Length (in inches)	$1\frac{1}{2}$	$2\frac{1}{2}$	2	$1\frac{3}{4}$	$1\frac{1}{4}$	$2\frac{1}{2}$	$1\frac{1}{2}$	$2\frac{3}{4}$

MODEL IT

You can use a number line to help you begin to draw the line plot.

The earthworms are measured to the nearest $\frac{1}{4}$ inch. So, the scale is $\frac{1}{4}$ inch.

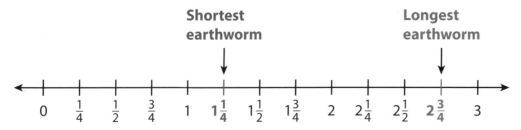

MODEL IT

You can use models to help you display the data.

The table shows how many earthworms there are of each length.

Each X stands for 1 earthworm.

$1\frac{1}{4}$ inches	X
$1\frac{1}{2}$ inches	XX
$1\frac{3}{4}$ inches	X
2 inches	X
$2\frac{1}{4}$ inches	
$2\frac{1}{2}$ inches	XX
$2\frac{3}{4}$ inches	X

CONNECT IT

Now you will use the problem from the previous page to help you understand how to display data in a line plot.

1 Complete the scale numbers on the line plot below. Use a scale of $\frac{1}{4}$ inch.

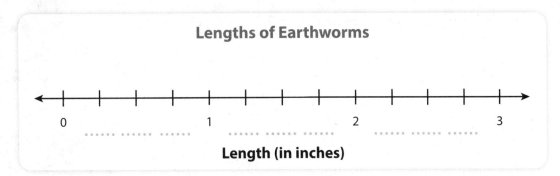

Lengths of Earthworms

0   1   2   3

Length (in inches)

2 How many worms did Brian measure? ....

3 There will be an X on the line plot for each earthworm. If two or more earthworms are the same length, the Xs will be drawn one above the other. How many Xs will be on the line plot? ....

4 How many worms are $1\frac{1}{4}$ inches long? .... Draw that many Xs above $1\frac{1}{4}$.

5 How many worms are $1\frac{1}{2}$ inches long? .... Draw that many Xs above $1\frac{1}{2}$.

6 Complete the line plot. Make sure to draw an X for each earthworm measurement.

7 Explain what each X on the line plot stands for.

8 REFLECT

Look back at your Try It, strategies by classmates, and Model Its. Which models or strategies do you like best for displaying data in a line plot? Explain.

....

....

....

....

APPLY IT

Use what you just learned to solve these problems.

9 Complete the line plot of the ribbon lengths data. Start by choosing a scale and labeling the scale numbers. Give the line plot a title.

Ribbon Lengths (in inches)							
3	$2\frac{1}{2}$	$2\frac{1}{2}$	$3\frac{1}{2}$	$4\frac{1}{2}$	3	$4\frac{1}{2}$	$4\frac{1}{2}$

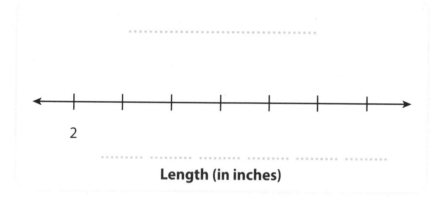

2

Length (in inches)

10 Draw a line plot of the data in the table. Start by choosing a scale and labeling the scale numbers. Give the line plot a title.

Plant Lengths								
Plant	A	B	C	D	E	F	G	H
Length (in inches)	$6\frac{1}{4}$	$6\frac{1}{2}$	$5\frac{3}{4}$	$6\frac{1}{2}$	$6\frac{3}{4}$	$6\frac{1}{4}$	$5\frac{3}{4}$	$6\frac{1}{2}$

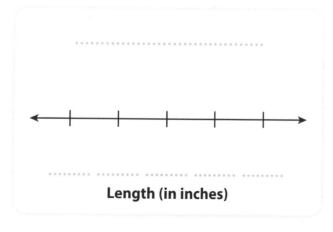

Length (in inches)

Practice Displaying Data in a Line Plot

Study the Example showing how to display data in a line plot.
Then solve problems 1–3.

EXAMPLE

Denise works in a candle shop. She measures and sorts the candles by length.
How can Denise make a line plot for these candle lengths?

Candle	A	B	C	D	E	F	G	H
Length (inches)	$2\frac{1}{4}$	$2\frac{3}{4}$	$2\frac{3}{4}$	$3\frac{1}{2}$	$3\frac{1}{2}$	3	$2\frac{1}{4}$	$3\frac{1}{2}$

Make a number line and mark
the candle lengths with Xs.

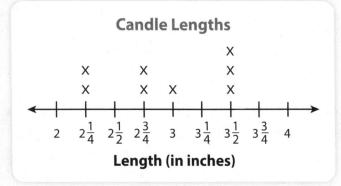

Candle Lengths

Length (in inches)

---

1 Denise measures more candles and records the lengths
in this list. Make a line plot to display the data in the list.
Use an X to stand for each candle. Give your line plot a title.

Candle Lengths (in inches)	
$8\frac{1}{2}$	$9\frac{1}{2}$
$8\frac{3}{4}$	10
$9\frac{1}{2}$	$8\frac{1}{2}$
10	10
$8\frac{1}{2}$	$8\frac{3}{4}$
10	$8\frac{1}{2}$
$9\frac{1}{2}$	10

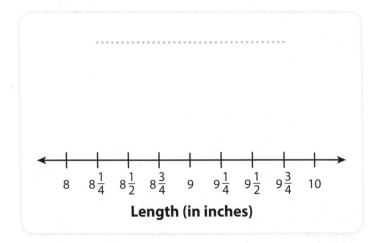

Length (in inches)

2 Some students measure the length of each other's hair. They record the data in this list. Make a line plot to display the data.

Hair Lengths (inches)							
$5\frac{1}{2}$	$5\frac{1}{4}$	$6\frac{1}{2}$	$5\frac{3}{4}$	$6\frac{1}{2}$	$5\frac{3}{4}$	7	7
$7\frac{1}{2}$	$5\frac{1}{4}$	$6\frac{1}{4}$	$7\frac{1}{4}$	$5\frac{3}{4}$	$7\frac{1}{4}$	$6\frac{1}{2}$	$7\frac{3}{4}$

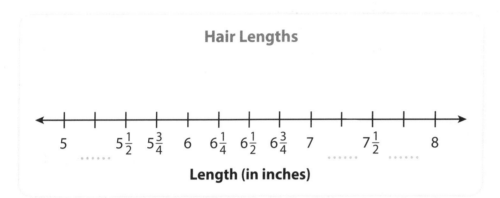

Hair Lengths

Length (in inches)

3 Jamal collects leaves for a science project. He records the lengths in this list. Make a line plot to display the data. Give your line plot a title.

Lengths of Leaves (inches)							
$3\frac{1}{4}$	$5\frac{1}{4}$	$4\frac{1}{4}$	$5\frac{1}{4}$	$4\frac{1}{2}$	$5\frac{1}{2}$	$3\frac{1}{4}$	$3\frac{1}{2}$
$5\frac{3}{4}$	$5\frac{1}{2}$	$4\frac{3}{4}$	$5\frac{1}{2}$	$5\frac{3}{4}$	$3\frac{1}{2}$	$5\frac{1}{2}$	$3\frac{3}{4}$

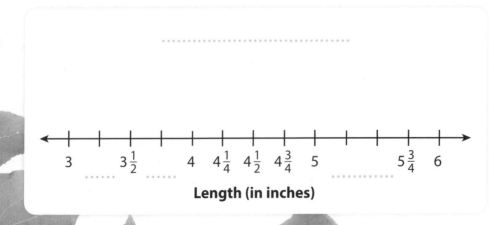

Length (in inches)

Refine Measuring Length and Plotting Data on Line Plots

Complete the Example below. Then solve problems 1–7.

EXAMPLE

In science club, Lily measures the lengths of dragonfly wings. She makes a line plot of her data shown below. Then she finds one more dragonfly wing.

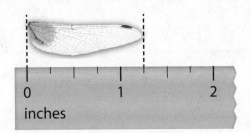

0   1   2
inches

Measure the wing to the nearest $\frac{1}{4}$ inch.

Add the last measurement to Lily's line plot. Which wing length appears most often on the line plot?

Look at how you could show your work using Lily's line plot.

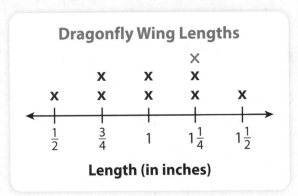

Dragonfly Wing Lengths

$\frac{1}{2}$ $\frac{3}{4}$ 1 $1\frac{1}{4}$ $1\frac{1}{2}$

Length (in inches)

Solution ....

The student lines up one end of the dragonfly wing with 0 on the ruler. Then the student finds the mark on the ruler closest to the other end of the wing.

PAIR/SHARE
How do you know which wing length appears most often?

APPLY IT

1 Use the line plot in the Example. How many dragonfly wings are shorter than 1 inch?

Solution ....

What does each X tell me?

PAIR/SHARE
Describe how you found the answer.

2 Lee measures the lengths of his friends' hands. He records the measurements in the table below. Complete the line plot below using Lee's data.

Hand Lengths						
Person	Arty	Leo	Meg	Olivia	Ruby	Zain
Length (in inches)	$5\frac{1}{2}$	5	$4\frac{3}{4}$	$5\frac{1}{2}$	5	$5\frac{3}{4}$

I can find the shortest measurement and the longest measurement to help me label my first and last scale numbers.

Hand Lengths

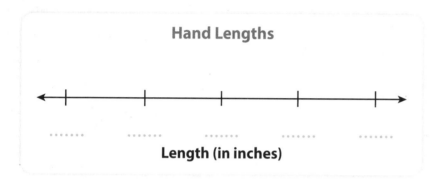

Length (in inches)

PAIR/SHARE
Is there an X above every number on your line plot? Why or why not?

3 Use a ruler to measure the marker. To the nearest half inch, how long is the marker?

How can I find the nearest half inch on the ruler?

Ⓐ 3 inches

Ⓑ $3\frac{1}{4}$ inches

Ⓒ $3\frac{1}{2}$ inches

Ⓓ $4\frac{1}{2}$ inches

Vicky chose Ⓑ as the correct answer. How did she get that answer?

PAIR/SHARE
Does Vicky's choice answer the question?

Use the line plot to solve problems 4 and 5.

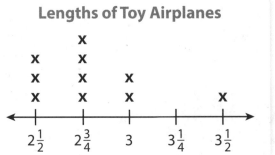

Lengths of Toy Airplanes

Length (in inches)

4 Which set of data was used to make the line plot? All data are in inches.

Ⓐ

$2\frac{1}{2}$	$2\frac{3}{4}$	3	$3\frac{1}{4}$	$3\frac{1}{2}$

Ⓑ

3	4	2	0	1

Ⓒ

$2\frac{1}{2}$	$2\frac{1}{2}$	$2\frac{1}{2}$	$2\frac{3}{4}$	$2\frac{3}{4}$
$2\frac{3}{4}$	$2\frac{3}{4}$	3	3	$3\frac{1}{2}$

Ⓓ

3	4	2	0	1
$2\frac{1}{2}$	$2\frac{3}{4}$	3	$3\frac{1}{4}$	$3\frac{1}{2}$

5 Tell whether each sentence is *True* or *False*.

	True	False
There are four airplanes shown on the line plot.	Ⓐ	Ⓑ
None of the airplanes measures $3\frac{1}{4}$ inches.	Ⓒ	Ⓓ
All of the planes are longer than 2 inches.	Ⓔ	Ⓕ
Exactly three planes measure $2\frac{3}{4}$ inches.	Ⓖ	Ⓗ

6 Use an inch ruler for this problem.

Leaf Lengths					
Leaf	A	B	C	D	E
Length (in inches)					

Part A Measure the leaves to the nearest one-fourth inch. Record the lengths in the table.

A

C

E

B

D

Part B Complete the line plot using the measurements you recorded in the table.

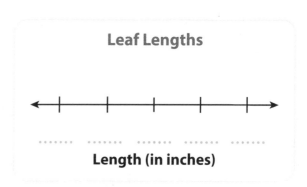

Leaf Lengths

Length (in inches)

7 MATH JOURNAL

Nia and Kyle are making a line plot for the inch measurements $3\frac{1}{2}$, 2, $2\frac{1}{4}$, 2, $2\frac{3}{4}$, 3, and $2\frac{3}{4}$. Nia says the number line could begin at 0 and end at 4. Kyle says it could begin at 2 and end at $3\frac{1}{2}$. Who is correct? Explain.

☑ **SELF CHECK** Go back to the Unit 4 Opener and see what you can check off.

In this unit you learned to . . .

Skill	Lesson
Use a fraction to show equal parts of a whole, for example: when a whole has 4 equal parts, each part is $\frac{1}{4}$ of the whole.	20, 21
Use a number line to show fractions and find a fraction on a number line.	21
Understand that equivalent fractions show the same amount and name the same point on a number line.	22
Find equivalent fractions, for example: fractions equivalent to $\frac{1}{2}$ include $\frac{2}{4}, \frac{3}{6}$, and $\frac{4}{8}$.	23
Write whole numbers as fractions, for example: $5 = \frac{5}{1}$ or $\frac{10}{2}$.	23
Compare fractions with the same numerator or the same denominator, including using $<, >$, and $=$, for example: $\frac{1}{3} > \frac{1}{8}$ and $\frac{4}{6} < \frac{5}{6}$.	24, 25
Measure length to the nearest $\frac{1}{2}$ or $\frac{1}{4}$ inch and show data on a line plot.	26

Think about what you learned.

Use words, numbers, and drawings.

1 One topic I could use in my everyday life is .... because . . .

2 The hardest thing I learned to do is .... because . . .

3 One thing I still need to work on is . . .

Use Fractions

Study an Example Problem and Solution

SMP 1 Make sense of problems and persevere in solving them.

Read this problem involving fractions. Then look at G.O.'s solution to this problem.

8-Mile Trail

G.O. is running on the 8-Mile Trail. At the welcome center, he finds trail plans.

Trail Plans

- Plant trees along the trail every fraction of a mile.

- Use a unit fraction greater than $\frac{1}{8}$ but less than $\frac{1}{2}$.

G.O. wants to find how many trees could be planted.

- Name a fraction that is greater than $\frac{1}{8}$ but less than $\frac{1}{2}$.

- Draw a number line from 0 to 8.

- Divide the sections between whole numbers to show your fraction.

- Label each mark with a whole number or fraction.

- Count all the marks from 0 to 8. Tell how many trees will be planted.

Read the sample solution on the next page. Then look at the checklist below. Find and mark parts of the solution that match the checklist.

 PROBLEM-SOLVING CHECKLIST

☐ Tell what is known.

☐ Tell what the problem is asking.

☐ Show all your work.

☐ Show that the solution works.

a. **Circle** something that is known.

b. **Underline** something that you need to find.

c. **Draw a box around** what you do to solve the problem.

d. **Put a checkmark** next to the part that shows the solution works.

G.O.'S SOLUTION

Hi, I'm G.O. Here's how I solved the problem.

- **First, I need to find a fraction that is greater than $\frac{1}{8}$ but less than $\frac{1}{2}$.**

  I think $\frac{1}{3}$ will work. I can draw same-sized models to check.

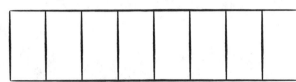 eighths

The denominator in $\frac{1}{3}$ tells me there are 3 equal parts.

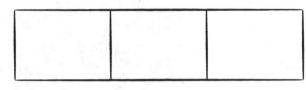 thirds

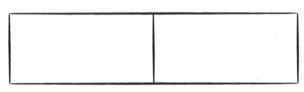 halves

The $\frac{1}{3}$ parts are bigger than the $\frac{1}{8}$ parts.

The $\frac{1}{3}$ parts are smaller than the $\frac{1}{2}$ parts.

So, $\frac{1}{3} > \frac{1}{8}$ and $\frac{1}{3} < \frac{1}{2}$.

- **Now I can make a number line.**

  I chose thirds, so I'll divide each section between whole numbers into three equal parts.

The number line goes to 8 because the trail is 8 miles long.

$0 \quad \frac{1}{3} \quad \frac{2}{3} \quad 1 \quad \frac{4}{3} \quad \frac{5}{3} \quad 2 \quad \frac{7}{3} \quad \frac{8}{3} \quad 3 \quad \frac{10}{3} \quad \frac{11}{3} \quad 4 \quad \frac{13}{3} \quad \frac{14}{3} \quad 5 \quad \frac{16}{3} \quad \frac{17}{3} \quad 6 \quad \frac{19}{3} \quad \frac{20}{3} \quad 7 \quad \frac{22}{3} \quad \frac{23}{3} \quad 8$

- **Start at 0 and count the marks.**

  There are 25 marks. So, 25 trees will be planted.

Try Another Approach

There are many ways to solve problems. Think about how you might solve the 8-Mile Trail problem in a different way.

8-Mile Trail

G.O. is running on the 8-Mile Trail. At the welcome center, he finds trail plans.

Trail Plans

- Plant trees along the trail every fraction of a mile.
- Use a unit fraction greater than $\frac{1}{8}$ but less than $\frac{1}{2}$.

G.O. wants to find how many trees could be planted.

- Name a fraction that is greater than $\frac{1}{8}$ but less than $\frac{1}{2}$.
- Draw a number line from 0 to 8.
- Divide the sections between whole numbers to show your fraction.
- Label each mark with a whole number or fraction.
- Count all the marks from 0 to 8. Tell how many trees will be planted.

PLAN IT

Answer these questions to help you start thinking about a plan.

A. What are some unit fractions greater than $\frac{1}{8}$?

B. Which of these fractions are less than $\frac{1}{2}$?

SOLVE IT

Find a different solution for the 8-Mile Trail problem. Show all your work on a separate sheet of paper.

You may want to use the Problem-Solving Tips to get started.

PROBLEM-SOLVING TIPS

- **Models**

- **Word Bank**

fraction	numerator	less than
equal parts	denominator	greater than

- **Sentence Starters**

- _____ is greater than _____

- The denominator tells me _____

☑ PROBLEM-SOLVING CHECKLIST

Make sure that you . . .
- ☐ tell what you know.
- ☐ tell what you need to do.
- ☐ show all your work.
- ☐ show that the solution works.

REFLECT

Use Mathematical Practices As you work through the problem, discuss these questions with a partner.

- **Use Structure** How can you use the denominators of unit fractions to compare them?

- **Reason Mathematically** How can you think about equal parts to find a unit fraction that is greater than or less than another unit fraction?

Discuss Models and Strategies

Read the problem. Write a solution on a separate sheet of paper. Remember, there can be lots of ways to solve a problem!

Flower Gardens

G.O. is helping to plant flowers near the 8-Mile Trail. He will plant two flower gardens at the welcome center. The gardens are circle shaped.

Here are the plans.

Flower Garden 1

- Divide the circle into equal parts. Make 2, 3, or 4 parts.

- Use a different color flower in each part.

Possible Diagrams for Garden 1

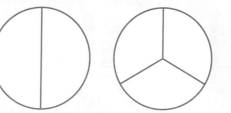

Flower Garden 2

- Divide the circle into equal parts. Make 6 or 8 parts.

- Use the same color flowers as Garden 1.

- The fraction of Garden 2 that has each color flower should be equivalent to Garden 1.

Possible Diagrams for Garden 2

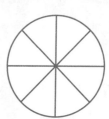

What two circles can G.O. use to draw a diagram of the gardens?

PLAN IT AND SOLVE IT
Find a solution for the Flower Gardens problem.

Follow the directions in the plan.

- Choose two circles that can be used to show equivalent fractions.

- Color the circles or label the sections with color names.

- Write a pair of equivalent fractions. Tell how you know they are equivalent.

You may want to use the Problem-Solving Tips to get started.

PROBLEM-SOLVING TIPS

- **Questions**

  - How many equal parts are shown in the circles?

  - What are some different ways to match up circles to show equivalent fractions?

- **Word Bank**

equivalent fractions	part	size
equal parts	whole	same

☑ **PROBLEM-SOLVING CHECKLIST**

Make sure that you . . .
- ☐ tell what you know.
- ☐ tell what you need to do.
- ☐ show all your work.
- ☐ show that the solution works.

REFLECT

Use Mathematical Practices As you work through the problem, discuss these questions with a partner.

- **Make an Argument** What are different ways to prove that two fractions are equivalent?

- **Use Models** How can you use the diagrams to help you solve the problem?

Persevere On Your Own

Read the problem. Write a solution on a separate sheet of paper.

Drinking Fountains

G.O. talks to a worker along the 8-Mile Trail. The worker is planning where to put new drinking fountains. Here is what the worker says.

- There will be 4, 6, or 8 drinking fountains.
- The trail will be divided into equal sections.
- One drinking fountain will be placed in the middle of each section.

Where should the drinking fountains be placed?

SOLVE IT

Help G.O. find the locations of the drinking fountains.

- Decide how many drinking fountains to use.

- Make a rectangular diagram of the trail.

- Divide the rectangle into equal parts. Make the same number of parts as drinking fountains.

- Write a fraction that names each part.

- Mark with a dot where each fountain will be.

REFLECT

Use Mathematical Practices After you complete the task, choose one of these questions to discuss with a partner.

- **Use Tools** What tools did you use to make the equal parts in the diagram? Tell how you used the tools.

- **Be Precise** What does the diagram show? Describe it to your partner. Use fractions, whole numbers, and measurement units to describe it.

Trail Signs

G.O. has an idea for signs to be put along the 8-Mile Trail. A sign at each mile marker tells what fraction of the whole trail people have completed.

The sign looks like this. The rectangle will be shaded to show the fraction. The blanks are for the mile number and fraction of the whole trail.

What would the completed signs look like?

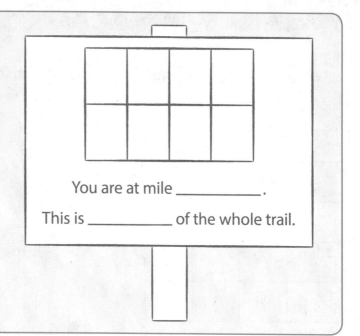

You are at mile _____.

This is _____ of the whole trail.

SOLVE IT

Help G.O. make drawings of the signs.

• Choose four mile markers along the 8-Mile Trail.

• Draw a sign for each mile marker you chose.

• Shade the rectangle and write numbers in the blanks.

REFLECT

Use Mathematical Practices After you complete the task, choose one of these questions to discuss with a partner.

• **Use Models** Look at the shaded models you made. How does each model relate to the words and numbers on the sign?

• **Reason with Numbers** What denominators did you use on your signs? Why?

1 Choose >, <, or = to compare each pair of fractions.

		>	<	=
$\frac{5}{8}$ ☐ $\frac{1}{8}$		Ⓐ	Ⓑ	Ⓒ
$\frac{1}{6}$ ☐ $\frac{1}{2}$		Ⓓ	Ⓔ	Ⓕ
$\frac{3}{4}$ ☐ $\frac{3}{6}$		Ⓖ	Ⓗ	Ⓘ
$\frac{4}{8}$ ☐ $\frac{1}{2}$		Ⓙ	Ⓚ	Ⓛ

2 Look at the number lines below.

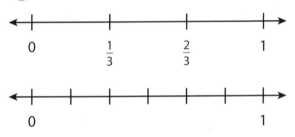

Decide if each statement is true.

Choose *True* or *False* for each statement.

	True	False
$\frac{0}{3} = \frac{0}{6}$	Ⓐ	Ⓑ
$\frac{1}{3} = \frac{1}{6}$	Ⓒ	Ⓓ
$\frac{2}{3} = \frac{4}{6}$	Ⓔ	Ⓕ
$\frac{3}{3} = \frac{3}{6}$	Ⓖ	Ⓗ

3 Which fractions are equivalent to 2? Choose all the correct answers.

Ⓐ $\frac{1}{2}$

Ⓑ $\frac{2}{1}$

Ⓒ $\frac{2}{2}$

Ⓓ $\frac{4}{2}$

Ⓔ $\frac{2}{4}$

4 Which statements about fractions are true? Choose all the correct answers.

Ⓐ Two fractions can be equivalent if they have different denominators.

Ⓑ A fraction that has the same number in both the numerator and denominator is equal to 1.

Ⓒ A fraction with the number 1 in the denominator is called a unit fraction.

Ⓓ All fractions are less than 1.

Ⓔ All fractions describe equal parts of a whole.

5 Use fractions from the box to label the points on the number line.

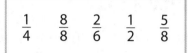

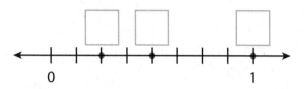

6 The lengths of ten strings are shown in the table.

Length (in.)	4	$4\frac{1}{4}$	$4\frac{1}{4}$	$4\frac{3}{4}$	$4\frac{1}{2}$	$4\frac{1}{4}$	$4\frac{1}{4}$	$4\frac{1}{2}$	$4\frac{3}{4}$	5

Part A Draw a line plot to show the lengths of the strings.

Part B Write two statements to describe the data in the line plot.

....

....

....

Performance Task

Answer the questions and show all your work on separate paper.

The owner of the neighborhood pizzeria, Itsa Pizza, would like you to draw diagrams to show the different combinations of toppings on 6 pizzas. Each diagram will show a rectangular pizza cut into 8 equal-sized pieces. She wants each pizza to be completely covered with toppings with no overlaps.

Fajita	$\frac{1}{2}$ pepper, $\frac{1}{2}$ onion
Deluxe	$\frac{1}{8}$ mushroom, $\frac{3}{8}$ olive, $\frac{1}{4}$ broccoli, $\frac{1}{4}$ pepper
Broc-Star	$\frac{5}{8}$ broccoli, $\frac{1}{8}$ onion, $\frac{1}{8}$ spinach
The Itsa Pizza	$\frac{2}{4}$ tomato, $\frac{1}{4}$ olive
Mighty Mush	$\frac{1}{4}$ spinach, $\frac{4}{8}$ mushroom, $\frac{2}{4}$ tomato
The Green Hula	$\frac{3}{4}$ onion, $\frac{3}{3}$ pineapple, $\frac{1}{4}$ broccoli

Checklist
Did you . . .
☐ draw a diagram for each pizza?
☐ show what each letter in your diagram means?
☐ check your calculations?

Use grid paper to draw diagrams of each pizza described above. If the toppings will not fully cover the pizza, add a new topping or change the amounts of the toppings shown. If the instructions list too many toppings, change the amounts of the toppings to make it work.

Here is an example for the Fajita pizza:

P	P	P	P	P = pepper
O	O	O	O	O = onion

REFLECT

Use Mathematical Practices After you complete the task, choose one of the following questions to answer.

- **Model** How did you decide how much of the pizza to cover with each topping?

- **Reason Mathematically** What are the different fractions listed that show half a pizza?

Vocabulary

Draw or write to show examples for each term. Then draw or write to show other math words in the unit.

denominator   the number below the line in a fraction that tells the number of equal parts in the whole.

My Example

equivalent fractions   two or more different fractions that name the same part of a whole or the same point on a number line.

My Example

fraction   a number that names equal parts of a whole. A fraction names a point on the number line.

My Example

mixed number   a number with a whole-number part and a fractional part.

My Example

numerator   the number above the line in a fraction that tells the number of equal parts that are being described.

My Example

unit fraction   a fraction with a numerator of 1. Other fractions are built from unit fractions.

My Example

My Word: _____
_____
_____

My Example

My Word: _____
_____
_____

My Example

My Word: _____
_____
_____

My Example

My Word: _____
_____
_____

My Example

My Word: _____
_____
_____

My Example

My Word: _____
_____
_____

My Example

☑ SELF CHECK

Before starting this unit, check off the skills you know below. As you complete each lesson, see how many more skills you can check off!

I can . . .	Before	After
Tell and write time to the nearest minute on digital clocks and clocks with hands and solve problems about time.	☐	☐
Estimate liquid volume and solve problems about liquid volume.	☐	☐
Estimate mass and solve problems about mass.	☐	☐

Build Your Vocabulary

REVIEW

AM hour hand

PM minute hand

Math Vocabulary

Draw the minute hand and hour hand to show the time written beside each one. Then list activities you do at each of these times and indicate if they are AM or PM activities.

Time	My Activities	AM or PM
2:35		
8:25		
11:45		
5:15		

Academic Vocabulary

Put a check next to the academic words you know. Then use the words to complete the sentences.

☐ restate ☐ record ☐ various ☐ frequently

1 There are .... strategies to help you tell time quickly and skip-counting counting by fives is one.

2 .... , cups are used to measure liquid in cooking recipes.

3 When I .... time, I pay close attention to where the hour and minute hands are on the clock.

4 I can .... what I say if you do not understand it the first time.

Time

Dear Family,

This week your child is learning to tell time to the nearest minute and to solve problems involving elapsed time.

To read time to the nearest minute, you find the hour first: Because the short hand has gone past the 3 and is not to the 4 yet, the hour on this clock is 3.

Then, to find the minutes past the hour, you start at the 12 and count by fives for each number (1, 2, 3, etc.) up to the number just before the minute hand (7). The number 7 marks 35 minutes past the hour. Then you count the 4 small marks past the 7 to the exact location of the minute hand, to get to 39. The time is 3:39.

Elapsed time is the amount of time that has passed between a start time and an end time. Here is one way to find elapsed time.

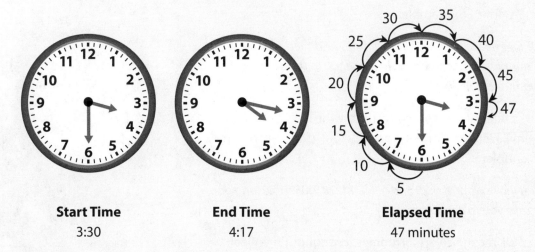

Start Time	**End Time**	**Elapsed Time**
3:30	4:17	47 minutes

Invite your child to share what he or she knows about telling time and finding elapsed time by doing the following activity together.

ACTIVITY SOLVING PROBLEMS ABOUT TIME

Do this activity with your child to practice finding elapsed time.

Work with your child to solve real-life problems about elapsed time. Talk with your child about activities you enjoy doing together and how much time they take.

Then create stories in which you know the start time and how long activities take (the elapsed time). Talk about how to find the end time. Discuss how to use a clock or a number line (like the one shown) to help find the end time. For example:

1. *Donna starts her swim lesson at 12:30. She warms up for 5 minutes. For 10 minutes she practices side breathing, and for 15 minutes she works on her freestyle stroke. When does her lesson end?*

Then create stories where you know how long activities take (the elapsed time) and the end time but need to find the start time. For example:

2. *Dinner needs to cook for 25 minutes and then cool for 5 minutes. What time should dinner go in the oven if you want to eat at 6:30?*

Finally, create stories where you know the start time and end time. Find how long the activity took (the elapsed time). For example:

3. *You leave work at 6:25 and get home at 7:05. How long does it take you to get home?*

Best of all, recognize opportunities throughout the week when you yourself are actually solving problems about time. Share these problems with your child to provide *actual* real-world practice!

Tick
Tic

Answers: **1.** 1:00; **2.** 6:00; **3.** 40 minutes

Explore **Working with Time**

In this lesson you will learn to tell time to the nearest minute and solve problems involving elapsed time. Use what you know to try to solve the problem below.

> **Lily starts reading a book after breakfast at the time shown on the clock. What time does the clock show?**

TRY IT

 **Math Toolkit**

• counters
• whiteboards
• clock faces
• sticky notes

DISCUSS IT

Ask your partner: Do you agree with me? Why or why not?

Tell your partner: A model I used was . . . It helped me . . .

CONNECT IT

1 LOOK BACK

Explain how you can find the time on the clock on the previous page.

2 LOOK AHEAD

Time is often given in terms of AM and PM, such as "Ted went to bed at 8:25 PM." You write AM for times from midnight until before noon and PM for times from noon until before midnight.

a. Write your answer to the problem on the previous page using AM or PM. Explain your choice.

b. Elapsed time is the time that has passed between a start time and an end time. Look at these clocks.

What is the start time? ....

What is the end time? ....

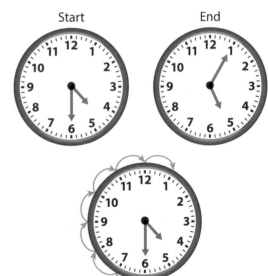

c. One way you could find the elapsed time in Part b is to **count by fives** on the start clock:

5, ..., ..., ..., ..., ..., ...

d. What is the elapsed time in Part b? ....

3 REFLECT

Sometimes a clock will use thick and thin marks instead of numbers. Explain how you can tell what time this clock shows.

Prepare for Working with Time

1 Think about what you know about time. Fill in each box. Use words, numbers, and pictures. Show as many ideas as you can.

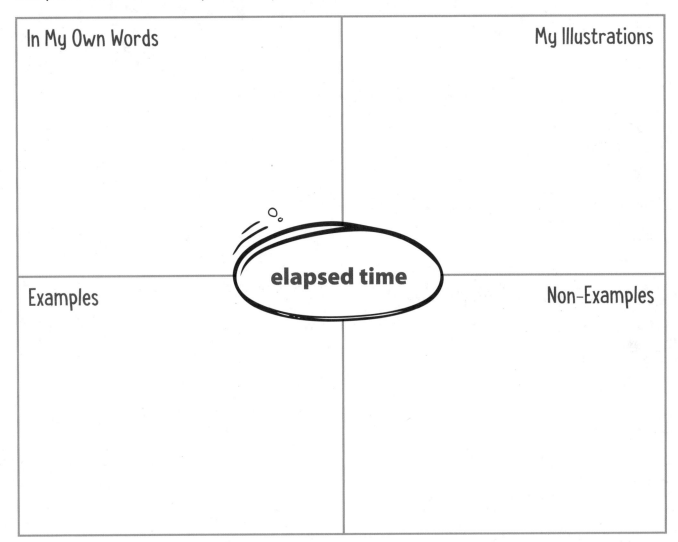

In My Own Words	My Illustrations

elapsed time

Examples	Non-Examples

2 Look at these clocks.

What is the start time? ....

What is the end time? ....

What is the elapsed time? ....

Start

End

3 Solve the problem. Show your work.

Brie starts watching a movie at the time shown on the clock. What time does the clock show?

Solution ....

4 Check your answer. Show your work.

Develop Telling Time to the Minute

Read and try to solve the problem below.

Sara sits down to eat lunch at 43 minutes past noon. At what time does Sara sit down to eat lunch? Include AM or PM in your answer.

TRY IT

 Math Toolkit
- counters
- whiteboards
- clock faces
- sticky notes

 **DISCUSS IT**

Ask your partner: Can you explain that again?

Tell your partner: I do not understand how . . .

Explore different ways to understand telling and writing time.

> **Sara sits down to eat lunch at 43 minutes past noon. At what time does Sara sit down to eat lunch? Include AM or PM in your answer.**

PICTURE IT
You can use a digital clock to show what time it is.

Noon is 12:00 PM. Sara sits down at 43 **minutes** past noon.

The clock shows PM because the time is from noon until before midnight.

MODEL IT
You can also use the next hour to tell what time it is.

Sara sits down to eat between 12:00 PM and 1:00 PM. You can tell the time by saying how many minutes after 12:00. You can also say how many minutes before 1:00.

To count the minutes, you always start at the **12**.

- **Count forward** to find out how many minutes after 12:00.

- **Count backward** from the 12 to find out how many minutes before 1:00.

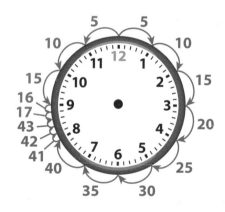

By counting backward, you can see that **43 minutes after 12:00 PM** describes the same time as **17 minutes before 1:00 PM**.

CONNECT IT

Now you will use the problem from the previous page to help you understand how to tell and write time.

1 Which hand on a clock shows the hour?

What two numbers should this hand be between to show the time Sara sits down to eat? Explain how you know.

2 Which hand on a clock shows the minutes? ....

How many minutes should this hand show? ....

3 At what time does Sara sit down to eat? ....

4 Draw the hands on the clock to show the time Sara sits down to eat.

5 Explain how to tell time to the minute on a clock with hands.

6 REFLECT

Look back at your **Try It**, strategies by classmates, and **Picture It** and **Model It**. Which models or strategies do you like best for telling time to the minute? Explain.

....

....

....

....

APPLY IT

Use what you just learned to solve these problems.

7 It is 7 minutes before 2 PM. Draw the hands on the clock at the right to show the time. Then write the time on the digital clock below. Be sure to include AM or PM.

8 Write the time shown in two different ways. Show your work.

Solution

9 Which phrases describe the time shown on the clock below?

Ⓐ 48 minutes after 5:00

Ⓑ 48 minutes before 5:00

Ⓒ 48 minutes before 6:00

Ⓓ 12 minutes before 5:00

Ⓔ 12 minutes before 6:00

Ⓕ 12 minutes after 6:00

Practice Telling Time to the Minute

**Study the Example showing how to tell time to the minute.
Then solve problems 1–9.**

EXAMPLE

What time does the clock show?

The hour hand shows that it is between 3 o'clock and
4 o'clock. It takes 5 minutes for the minute hand to
move from one number to the next. It takes 1 minute
for the minute hand to move from one mark to the next.

Count by fives from the 12 to the 7. Then **count 2 more**
minutes.

The clock shows 37 minutes after 3, or 3:37.

 Look at the red arrows on the outside of the clock. Count by fives and
by ones to find the minutes before 4:00. Fill in the blanks.

5, 10, ..., ..., 21, ..., ...

.... minutes before ....

Write the time in two ways in problems 2 and 3.

....

.... minutes before ....

....

.... minutes before ....

Write the time on the digital clocks in problems 4 and 5 so that each pair of clocks shows the same time.

4

5

Draw the hands on the clocks in problems 6 and 7 to show the time.

6 It is 13 minutes after 4.

7 It is 13 minutes before 7.

8 Write the time in three ways.

....

.... minutes after ....

.... minutes before ....

9 Look at the clock in problem 8. Draw hands on the clock below to show what time it will be in 24 minutes.

Develop Finding the End Time in Word Problems

Read and try to solve the problem below.

> Jenna gets home from school at 3:30 PM. She does math homework for 10 minutes. Next she does science homework for 15 minutes. Then she practices the piano for 22 minutes. What time does Jenna finish?

TRY IT

 **Math Toolkit**
- base-ten blocks
- connecting cubes
- clock faces
- 1-centimeter grid paper
- sticky notes

DISCUSS IT

Ask your partner: Why did you choose that strategy?

Tell your partner: The strategy I used to find the answer was . . .

Explore different ways to understand finding the end time in word problems.

> Jenna gets home from school at 3:30 PM. She does math homework for 10 minutes. Next she does science homework for 15 minutes. Then she practices the piano for 22 minutes. What time does Jenna finish?

PICTURE IT

You can use a clock to help you find the end time.

The first clock shows 3:30, because that is when Jenna starts her homework. Count **10 minutes** for her math homework, **15 minutes** for her science homework, and **22 minutes** for her piano practice.

The second clock shows the time Jenna finishes.

MODEL IT

You can also use a number line to help you find the end time.

The number line below shows times in hours and minutes. Each long mark shows 5 minutes. Each short mark shows 1 minute.

Start at 3:30. Show a jump on the number line for each task. Each jump is equal to the number of minutes it takes Jenna to do the task.

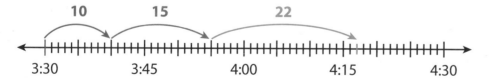

The last jump ends at the time Jenna finishes all three tasks.

CONNECT IT
Now you will use the problem from the previous page to help you understand how to find the end time in word problems.

1 Explain how to figure out the total elapsed time from the number of minutes Jenna spends doing her homework and practicing the piano.

2 Explain how you can use the total elapsed time to find Jenna's end time for doing her homework and practicing the piano.

3 What time does Jenna finish? .... Why did the hour number change?

4 Explain how to find the end time when you know the start time and the total elapsed time.

5 REFLECT

Look back at your **Try It**, strategies by classmates, and **Picture It** and **Model It**. Which models or strategies do you like best for finding the end time in word problems? Explain.

....

....

....

....

APPLY IT

Use what you just learned to solve these problems.

6 Nate finishes dinner at 7:10 PM. He does dishes for 15 minutes and then takes a shower for 10 minutes. Then he reads for 15 minutes before he goes to bed. What time does Nate go to bed? Show your work.

Solution ....

7 Kari starts a phone call to her family at 11:45 AM. She talks to her grandma for 10 minutes, then her grandpa for 5 minutes, and then her cousin for 8 minutes. What time does Kari end the call? Use the number line to show your work.

11:45   12:00   12:15

Solution ....

8 Rashid makes a stuffed bear at the toy store. He starts at 4:40 PM. He spends 25 minutes at the stuffing table and 21 minutes at the decorating table before he is done. What time does he finish? Show your work.

Solution ....

Practice Finding the End Time in Word Problems

Study the Example showing how to find the end time when you know the start time and the elapsed time. Then solve problems 1–6.

EXAMPLE

Anna starts walking her dog, Pickles, at 2:40 PM. She walks for 25 minutes. Then she plays ball with Pickles for 15 minutes. What time does Anna finish?

Start at 2:40. Count **25 minutes** for the walk. Then count **15 minutes** for playing ball. The minute hand goes past 12, so the hour moves ahead to the 3. The minute hand ends on the 4.

The second clock shows the end time, which is 3:20 PM.

1. Alma goes to the playground at 2:45 PM. She spends 20 minutes on the swings and 10 minutes on the jungle gym. She plays on the slide for 12 minutes. Then she goes home. What time does Alma go home? Fill in the blanks.

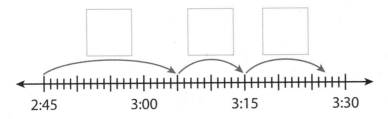

2:45   3:00   3:15   3:30

Alma goes home at ....

2. Juanita gets in line for the Safari Ride at 11:55 AM. She waits in line for 8 minutes. The ride lasts 7 minutes. What time does she get off the ride?

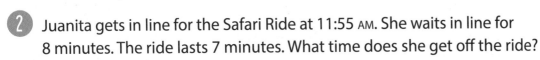

11:45   12:00   12:15

Solution ....

3 Jay goes outside at 10:50 AM and spends 35 minutes looking for worms. Then he takes 10 minutes to collect his gear before leaving to go fishing. What time does Jay leave to go fishing? Draw hands on the blank clock to show the time. Write the time.

Jay leaves to go fishing at ....

4 Kareem starts climbing on the rock wall at 5:20 PM. He climbs for 16 minutes. What time does Kareem finish climbing on the rock wall?

5:15   5:30   5:45

Solution ....

5 The Mendoza family leaves home at 10:30 AM. They drive 25 minutes and stop at the store. The family spends 20 minutes in the store. Then they drive another 13 minutes to get to the beach. What time do they get to the beach? Show your work.

Solution ....

6 Sharna leaves school at 3:10 PM. It takes 12 minutes for her to walk home from school. It takes 7 minutes for her to gather her soccer equipment and 10 more minutes to get to the soccer field. Soccer practice starts at 3:45 PM. Sharna thinks she will be late. Do you agree? Explain.

Develop Finding the Start Time in Word Problems

Read and try to solve the problem below.

Marc's guitar lesson starts at 5:20 PM. It takes Marc 15 minutes to get to his lesson from his house. Before Marc leaves, he has to do chores for 25 minutes. What is the latest time Marc should start doing his chores to get to his lesson on time?

TRY IT

Math Toolkit
- connecting cubes
- clock faces
- 1-centimeter grid paper
- sticky notes

DISCUSS IT

Ask your partner: How did you get started?

Tell your partner: I started by . . .

Explore different ways to understand finding the start time in word problems.

> **Marc's guitar lesson starts at 5:20 PM. It takes Marc 15 minutes to get to his lesson from his house. Before Marc leaves, he has to do chores for 25 minutes. What is the latest time Marc should start doing his chores to get to his lesson on time?**

PICTURE IT

You can use a clock to help you find the start time.

The clock shows 5:20, because that is when Marc's guitar lesson starts. Count **15 minutes** backward for the time it takes to get to his lesson. Then count **25 minutes** backward for the time it takes him to do his chores.

The second clock shows the latest time Marc should start doing his chores.

MODEL IT

You can also use a number line to help you find the start time.

The number line below is like the one used previously to find an end time. It shows times in hours and minutes. Each long mark shows 5 minutes. Each short mark shows 1 minute.

Start at 5:20. Count back the number of minutes it takes Marc to get to his lesson and do his chores.

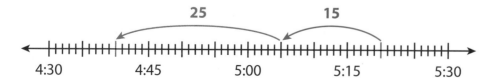

CONNECT IT

Now you will use the problem from the previous page to help you understand how to find the start time in word problems.

1 Explain why the times are counted backward from 5:20 on the clock and on the number line.

2 What is the latest time Marc should start doing his chores? ....

Why did the hour number change?

3 Explain how to find the start time when you know the end time and the elapsed time.

4 REFLECT

Look back at your **Try It**, strategies by classmates, and **Picture It** and **Model It**. Which models or strategies do you like best for finding the start time in word problems? Explain.

....

....

....

....

APPLY IT

Use what you just learned to solve these problems.

5 Mira finishes making fruit slices and sandwiches for lunch at 12:30 PM. She cut up fruit for 10 minutes and made sandwiches for 7 minutes. What time did she start making lunch? Use the number line to show your work.

12:00   12:15   12:30   12:45   1:00

Solution ....

6 Carter finishes cleaning his room at 11:35 AM. It took him 10 minutes to put away all his toys and 4 minutes to make his bed. What time did Carter start cleaning his room? Show your work.

Solution ....

7 Enrique walks 5 minutes from his grandma's house to the store, stops at the store for 20 minutes, and then walks 10 minutes from the store to his house. He gets to his house at 6:00 PM. What time did he leave his grandma's house? Show your work.

Solution ....

Practice Finding the Start Time in Word Problems

Study the Example showing how to find the start time when you know the end time and the elapsed time. Then solve problems 1–5.

EXAMPLE

Ming is riding her bike to Carmen's house. She wants to be there by 4:30 PM. First, she has to do homework for 30 minutes. The bike ride takes 15 minutes. What is the latest time Ming should start her homework?

Start at 4:30. Count back **15 minutes** for the bike ride. Then count back **30 minutes** for homework. The minute hand goes past 12, so the hour moves back to 3. The minute hand ends on the 9.

The second clock shows the start time, which is 3:45. The latest Ming should start her homework is 3:45 PM.

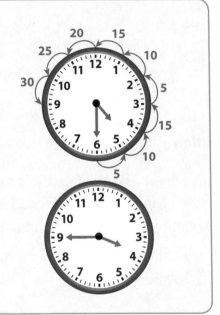

1. Johanna and her mom want to get to a birthday party at 2:00 PM. It is a 25-minute walk. On the way, they plan to stop for 15 minutes to get a card. What is the latest time they should leave? Show how to count backward on the number line.

1:15   1:30   1:45   2:00

Solution ....

2. If Johanna and her mom drive to the party in problem 1, it will take 8 minutes to get there. They still plan to stop and get a card. What is the latest time they should leave if they drive? Explain.

3 A movie starts at 5:15 PM. Rudy wants to get to the theater 25 minutes before the movie starts. It takes 10 minutes to drive to the theater. What time should Rudy leave home? Show your work.

Solution

4 Carlos plays basketball on the playground for 12 minutes. Then he swims at the pool for 25 minutes. He finishes at 12:00 PM. What time did he start playing basketball? Show your work.

Solution

5 Allie is done with gymnastics practice at 7:30 PM. At practice, she tumbled for 20 minutes. Then she worked on the balance beam for 10 minutes. Allie also practiced on the trampoline for 15 minutes. What time did she start practice? Show your work.

Solution

Refine Understanding of Time

Complete the Example below. Then solve problems 1–8.

EXAMPLE

Malea's soccer game starts at 9:40 AM and ends at 10:32 AM. How long is Malea's soccer game?

Look at how you could show your work.

9:40 is 20 minutes before 10:00.

10:32 is 32 minutes after 10:00.

20 + 32 = **52**

Solution ....

The student used what she knew about telling time before and after the hour to find the answer.

PAIR/SHARE
How else could you have solved this problem?

APPLY IT

1 Lamar watches his little sister while his mom is busy. He plays blocks with her for 15 minutes, peek-a-boo for 5 minutes, and trains for 13 minutes. His mom comes back to put his sister down for a nap at 2:15 PM. What time did Lamar start watching his sister? Show your work.

Do you need to count minutes forward or backward from 2:15 to find the time he started watching his sister?

PAIR/SHARE
How did you decide how you would solve the problem?

Solution ....

2 Mr. Chen starts doing yard work at 10:00 AM. He waters flowers for 6 minutes, weeds his garden for 12 minutes, and trims bushes for 27 minutes. What time is Mr. Chen done with his yard work? Show your work.

> I think adding all of the times together first would make this problem easier to solve.

PAIR/SHARE
Did you need to draw a clock or number line to help you? Why or why not?

Solution ....

3 Luca starts cleaning his room at the time shown on the clock.

Which tells the time shown on the clock?

Ⓐ 9 minutes before 9:00

Ⓑ 9 minutes before 10:00

Ⓒ 11 minutes before 10:00

Ⓓ 51 minutes before 9:00

Bo chose Ⓓ as the correct answer. How did he get that answer?

> All of the choices tell the time before the hour. What do you need to do to figure that out?

PAIR/SHARE
Does Bo's answer make sense?

4 Which pair of clocks shows the same time?

Ⓐ
Ⓑ
Ⓒ
Ⓓ

5 Patty, Joyce, and Stef need to leave for school at 7:45 AM.
Will each girl leave for school on time?

	Yes	No
Patty gets up at 7:10 AM. It takes her 10 minutes to get ready, 7 minutes to pack her lunch, and 15 minutes to eat breakfast.	Ⓐ	Ⓑ
Joyce gets up at 6:50 AM and exercises for 30 minutes. Then it takes her 20 minutes to get ready and 12 minutes to eat breakfast.	Ⓒ	Ⓓ
Stef gets up at 7:15 AM. It takes her 15 minutes to get ready, 5 minutes to pack her lunch, and 9 minutes to eat breakfast.	Ⓔ	Ⓕ

6 Mariah plays two games of checkers with her brother. The first game takes 12 minutes, and the second game takes 18 minutes. They put the game away at 7:55 PM. What time did they start playing checkers? Show your work.

They started playing checkers at ....

7 Jamal starts writing thank-you notes at 5:25 PM. It takes him 20 minutes to write them. He also spends some time writing addresses on the envelopes. He finishes at 6:00 PM. How long did it take Jamal to write the addresses? Show your work.

It took Jamal .... minutes to write the addresses.

8 MATH JOURNAL

Write a word problem about elapsed time that you can solve. Show how to find the answer.

✓ SELF CHECK   Go back to the Unit 5 Opener and see what you can check off.

Liquid Volume

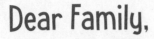

Dear Family,

This week your child is learning about measuring liquid volume using liters.

Liquid volume is the amount of space a liquid takes up.

One standard unit used to measure liquid volume is called a liter. A **liter** is about the same amount as a quart. It is helpful to picture about how much a liter is. A liter is approximately:

the amount of water in a large water bottle

the amount of milk in 4 small milk cartons

the amount of milk in $\frac{1}{4}$ of a gallon

Your child will use addition, subtraction, multiplication, and division to solve word problems related to liquid volume.

For example, the short yellow lines on this water jug show sections that each hold 1 liter. There are 8 sections, so the container holds a total of 8 liters when full.

If this 8-liter container is filled with juice, and 4 teams want to share it equally, how many liters of juice will each team get?

Your child might write equations like these to solve this problem:

$$8 \div 4 = ? \quad \text{or} \quad 4 \times ? = 8$$

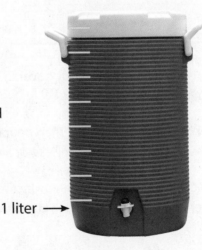

1 liter →

Invite your child to share what he or she knows about measuring liquid in liters by doing the following activity together.

ACTIVITY LIQUID VOLUME

Do this activity with your child to explore liquid volume.

Go on a scavenger hunt to find containers that hold *about one liter*, *less than one liter*, and *more than one liter*. Record the containers on the table below.

Some containers you might find are a flower vase, a baby food jar, a garbage can, or a paper cup. Any of these can be a good start to your list.

About one liter	Less than one liter	More than one liter

If you have a 1-liter (or 1 quart) plastic beverage bottle or yogurt container, use it to check your thinking.

- Fill the liter bottle with water and then pour into each container to check whether the container holds more, less, or almost the same amount.

- Make the activity more challenging by first estimating how many liters each of the larger objects holds, and then check your estimates!

Explore Working with Liquid Volume

In the previous lesson you learned about measuring time using minutes and hours. You can also measure liquid volume. Use what you know to try to solve the problem below.

Suppose you have a ruler and a 1 liter measuring cup. Explain which tool you would choose to measure the amount of water the bucket can hold and how you would use it.

TRY IT

Math Toolkit

- rulers
- cups
- 1-centimeter grid paper
- sticky notes

DISCUSS IT

Ask your partner: Do you agree with me? Why or why not?

Tell your partner: I agree with you about . . . because . . .

CONNECT IT

1 LOOK BACK

Explain which tool best measures the amount of water the bucket can hold.

2 LOOK AHEAD

When you measure how much water is in a bucket, you measure **liquid volume**. A **liter** is a standard unit of liquid volume. Each example below shows containers that hold about a liter.

a large water bottle

4 small milk cartons

$\frac{1}{4}$ of a gallon

a. Circle the container below that holds about a liter. Box the container that holds less than a liter. Put an X on the container that holds more than a liter.

b. Look at the container you crossed out in Part a. How can you find how many liters this container can hold when full?

3 REFLECT

Name a different container that holds less than 1 liter, one that holds about 1 liter, and one that holds more than 1 liter.

....

....

Prepare for Working with Liquid Volume

1 Think about what you know about measurement. Fill in each box. Use words,
   numbers, and pictures. Show as many ideas as you can.

Word	In My Own Words	Example
liquid volume		
liter		

2 Circle the container below that has a liquid volume of about a liter. Box the
   container that has a liquid volume less than a liter. Put an X on the container
   that has a liquid volume more than a liter.

3 Solve the problem. Show your work.

Suppose you have a ruler and a 1 liter measuring cup. Explain which tool you would choose to measure the amount of water the pitcher can hold and how you would use it.

Solution

4 Check your answer. Show your work.

Develop Estimating Liquid Volume

Read and try to solve the problem below.

> Kayla will use a liter carton to fill her small fish tank. Estimate how many liters of water the fish tank can hold when full.

1 liter

TRY IT

 **Math Toolkit**
- connecting cubes
- grid paper
- sticky notes

DISCUSS IT

Ask your partner: Why did you choose that strategy?

Tell your partner: The strategy I used to find the answer was . . .

Explore different ways to understand estimating liquid volume.

> Kayla will use a liter carton to fill her small fish tank. Estimate how many liters of water the fish tank can hold when full.

1 liter

PICTURE IT

You can use a model to help you estimate.

You can picture how many liter cartons would fit inside the fish tank.

Front View

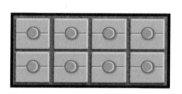

Top View

Count the number of cartons. This is your estimate.

MODEL IT

You can model the problem in another way to help you estimate.

This shows 1 liter of water in the fish tank.

You can think about what fraction of the fish tank is filled when it has 1 liter of water in it.

CONNECT IT

Now you will use the problem from the previous page to help you understand how to estimate liquid volume.

1 Look at the 1 liter of water shown in the fish tank in Model It. Explain how to find the fraction of the fish tank that is filled with water.

2 Explain how you can use this fraction to estimate how many liters of water the fish tank holds when full.

3 About how many liters of water does the fish tank hold when full?

4 Now look at the picture of the cartons inside the fish tank in Picture It.

Is your estimate close to the estimate this picture shows? ....

5 Explain how to estimate the number of liters of water it would take to fill a container.

6 REFLECT

Look back at your Try It, strategies by classmates, and Picture It and Model It. Which models or strategies do you like best for estimating liquid volume? Explain.

....

....

....

....

APPLY IT

Use what you just learned to solve these problems.

7 Estimate the liquid volume of the red container. Show your work.

1 liter

Solution ....

8 Estimate the liquid volume of the metal pan.

1 liter

Solution ....

9 Which could hold about 10 liters when full?

  Ⓐ a tea pot

  Ⓑ a water glass

  Ⓒ a bathtub

  Ⓓ a bathroom sink

Practice Estimating Liquid Volume

Study the Example showing how to estimate liquid volume. Then solve problems 1–7.

EXAMPLE

Jan is going to pour water in a picnic cooler. She is trying to estimate how many liters it can hold when it is full.

It looks like the cooler can hold six 1-liter bottles.

Jan estimates the cooler will hold about 6 liters of water.

1 liter

---

1   The bottle of juice holds 1 liter. About how many liters could the pitcher hold when full? How did you decide?

1 liter   ? liters

2   Which items could hold about 1 liter of water when full?

   Ⓐ a trash can   Ⓑ a bathtub

   Ⓒ a coffee pot   Ⓓ a flower vase

   Ⓔ a paper cup   Ⓕ a teaspoon

3   A kitchen sink holds about 40 liters of water. What could hold more than 40 liters of water?

   Ⓐ a bathtub   Ⓑ a cooking pot

   Ⓒ a coffee cup   Ⓓ a cereal bowl

4 This juice dispenser has 3 liters of juice in it. About how many liters does this juice dispenser hold when it is full?

Ⓐ 2 liters

Ⓑ 3 liters

Ⓒ 6 liters

Ⓓ 10 liters

5 About how many liters of water can the watering can hold when full?

Ⓐ $\frac{1}{2}$ liter

Ⓑ 1 liter

Ⓒ 2 liters

Ⓓ 5 liters

1 liter   ? liters

6 Explain how you estimated the answer to problem 5.

7 Explain how to estimate the fraction of the watering can in problem 5 that can be filled with 1 liter of water.

Develop Solving Word Problems About Liquid Volume

Read and try to solve the problem below.

> Maria has a cooler full of 8 liters of lemonade. She wants to put the lemonade into pitchers to place on the tables at her party. Each pitcher holds 2 liters. How many pitchers does Maria need?

TRY IT

 Math Toolkit
- counters
- buttons
- cups
- 1-centimeter grid paper
- sticky notes

DISCUSS IT

Ask your partner: Why did you choose that strategy?

Tell your partner: The strategy I used to find the answer was . . .

Explore different ways to understand solving word problems about liquid volume.

> Maria has a cooler full of 8 liters of lemonade. She wants to put the lemonade into pitchers to place on the tables at her party. Each pitcher holds 2 liters. How many pitchers does Maria need?

PICTURE IT
You can use a model to help you solve the problem.

The model below shows the cooler full of lemonade. Each mark on the left side of the cooler shows 1 liter. Each full line marks off a 2-liter section.

1 liter →

← 2 liters

MODEL IT
You can model the problem in another way to help you solve it.

Each pitcher holds 2 liters. The pitchers need to hold 8 liters of lemonade in all.

2 liters   2 liters   2 liters   2 liters

CONNECT IT

Now you will use the problem from the previous page to help you understand how to solve word problems about liquid volume.

1 How does the picture of the cooler in **Picture It** show you how many liters of lemonade a full cooler can hold?

How can you use the cooler to figure out how many pitchers are needed?

2 What do you need to do to find the number of pitchers Maria needs?

3 Write a division equation using *p* for the unknown in the problem. Then write a related multiplication equation. Then solve the equations.

4 A complete answer includes a label showing what is being counted. Write the answer to the problem, including a label. Why is it important to include a label?

5 REFLECT

Look back at your **Try It**, strategies by classmates, and **Picture It** and **Model It**. Which models or strategies do you like best for solving problems about liquid volume? Explain.

....

....

....

APPLY IT

Use what you just learned to solve these problems.

6 How much less water is in the second container than in the first container? Show your work.

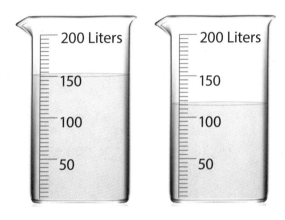

Solution ....

7 Ethan has 7 pitchers. Each pitcher contains 3 liters of water. How much water does Ethan have in all? Show your work.

Solution ....

8 Leo needs 12 liters of juice for a party. How many 2-liter bottles of juice should he buy? Show your work.

Solution ....

Practice Solving Word Problems About Liquid Volume

Study the Example showing how to solve a word problem about liquid volume. Then solve problems 1–8.

EXAMPLE

Bridget fills 7 water coolers for the school picnic. Each cooler holds 9 liters of water. How many liters of water are in all the coolers?

Each cooler has the same amount of water, so you can multiply to find the total.

$7 \times 9 = 63$

The coolers hold 63 liters of water.

1. Jose has a cooler with 25 liters of lemonade to take to school for his birthday party. Then he pours 1 liter from the cooler to keep at home. How many liters are left to take to school?

2. Ms. Lyon brought a cooler with 24 liters of lemonade to school to serve her students. The students are sitting at 8 different tables. She gives the same amount of lemonade to students at each table. How many liters does each table get?

3. Write a division equation with an unknown to show how you solved problem 2.

4 Samuel takes 5 full coolers of water like the one shown to his basketball game. How many liters of water altogether did he take to the game? Show your work.

1 liter ⟶{

Solution

5 Look at problem 4. If 3 coolers are completely empty after the game, how many liters of water are left? Show your work.

Solution

6 The fuel tank in Janice's car holds 60 liters of gas. She has 20 liters of gas in her tank. How much more gas does she need to fill up the tank? Show your work.

Solution

7 Bobby's aquarium holds 32 liters of water. He uses a 4-liter bucket to fill the tank. How many buckets of water are needed to fill the tank? Show your work.

Solution

8 Terry has pitchers that hold 2 liters and 5 liters. How can he use these pitchers to measure out exactly 3 liters of water?

Refine Understanding of Liquid Volume

Complete the Example below. Then solve problems 1–9.

EXAMPLE

Bella needs to prepare containers of water just like the one shown. How many liters of water will Bella need to prepare 7 such containers?

Look at how you could show your work using an equation.

Each container will hold 10 liters of water.

$7 \times 10 = 70$

Solution ....

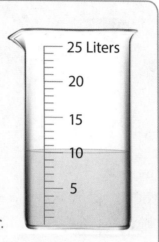

The student first needed to figure out how much water goes in each container.

PAIR/SHARE
How else could you solve this problem?

APPLY IT

1 Perry has 3 large barrels that collect rain water he uses to water his garden on dry days. After a recent storm, one barrel held 186 liters of water, one held 203 liters, and one held 190 liters. How many liters of collected rain water does Perry have in all? Show your work.

You need to find how many liters in all. What operation can you use to solve the problem?

PAIR/SHARE
How did you decide which information was important in the problem?

Solution ....

2 Mary pours the fruit juice from a 1-liter bottle into a large container. The large container with the 1 liter of fruit juice in it is shown below. Estimate the liquid volume of the large container.

You could think about how many 1-liter bottles would fit in the large container, or you could look at what fraction of the large container is filled by 1 liter of juice.

Solution ....

PAIR/SHARE
What strategy did you use to estimate the liquid volume?

3 Jason keeps his turtle in a tank that holds 20 liters of water. He keeps his frog in a tank that holds 10 liters of water. How much greater is the volume of the turtle tank than the frog tank?

Ⓐ 2 liters

Ⓑ 10 liters

Ⓒ 30 liters

Ⓓ 200 liters

Maya chose Ⓒ as the correct answer. How did she get that answer?

You need to find out how much more water one tank can hold than the other. How can you do that?

PAIR/SHARE
Does Maya's answer make sense?

4 This pot contains 1 liter of water. Which is the best estimate for how many liters the pot could hold when full?

Ⓐ 2 liters

Ⓑ 3 liters

Ⓒ 6 liters

Ⓓ 10 liters

5 Noah uses a full 8 liters of water to water 4 flower beds. He uses the same amount of water on each bed. How many liters of water does he use on each flower bed?

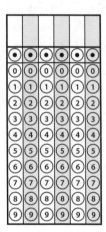

6 How many liters of water in total are these containers holding? Show your work.

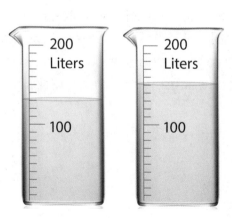

Solution ....

7 Which containers hold less than 1 liter when full?

Ⓐ kitchen sink

Ⓑ juice box

Ⓒ baby food jar

Ⓓ bathtub

Ⓔ paper cup

8 Molly fills a tub for her dog using a 4-liter bucket. She fills the bucket 6 times. How much water does Molly use to wash her dog? Show your work.

.... liters

9 MATH JOURNAL

One water truck holds 456 liters of water. Another water truck holds 325 liters of water. How many liters of water do the two trucks hold altogether? Explain how you found your answer using pictures, words, or equations.

✓ SELF CHECK Go back to the Unit 5 Opener and see what you can check off.

Mass

Dear Family,

This week your child is learning about measuring the mass of objects using units of grams or kilograms.

When people talk about measuring the **mass** of an object, they mean they are finding how much matter the object contains. One way to measure the mass of an object is to measure how heavy it is.

Two units commonly used to measure mass are **grams** and **kilograms**.

- The mass of a paper clip is about 1 gram.

- The mass of a wooden baseball bat is about 1 kilogram.

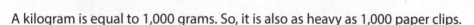

A kilogram is equal to 1,000 grams. So, it is also as heavy as 1,000 paper clips.

One way to find the mass of an object is to use a balance scale. In the picture, two 1-kilogram weights balance the bag of flour, showing that the mass of the flour is equal to 2 kilograms.

If you only want to estimate the approximate mass of something, one way to do that is to compare it to something else that you know the mass of. For example, if you lift these two books, they may seem to be about as heavy as the bag of flour. Since you know the bag of flour has a mass of 2 kilograms, you can estimate that the mass of the books is also about 2 kilograms. So, the mass of one book is about 1 kilogram.

Invite your child to share what he or she knows about measuring mass by doing the following activity together.

ACTIVITY MASS SCAVENGER HUNT

Do this activity with your child to explore mass.

Go on a scavenger hunt to find objects that have a mass of about 1 gram and objects that have a mass of about 1 kilogram. Record the objects on the table below.

Remember,

- 1 **gram** is about the mass of a paper clip.
- 1 **kilogram** is about the mass of a wooden baseball bat.

Some objects you might find are a rubber band, a library book, a dollar bill, a paper cup, a bag of rice. Any of these can be a good start to your list.

About 1 gram	More than 1 gram and less than 1 kilogram	About 1 kilogram

If you have a full one-liter bottle of water, or a full quart-sized container of yogurt, those items are very close to 1 kilogram in mass. You may also have a 1-kilogram dumbbell. You can use any of those items to help you compare the mass of each object on your list to 1 kilogram.

Explore Working with Mass

Previously you learned about measuring liquid volume. You can also measure an object's mass. Use what you know to try to solve the problem below.

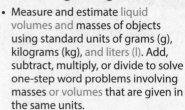
The paper clip measures about 1 gram on a scale. How could you estimate the mass of the pencil? How could you use paper clips to measure the mass of the pencil?

TRY IT

Math Toolkit
• pan balance
• 1-centimeter grid paper
• paper clips
• string
• paper plates

DISCUSS IT

Ask your partner: Can you explain that again?

Tell your partner:
I knew . . . so I . . .

CONNECT IT

1 LOOK BACK

Explain how you could estimate and measure the mass of the pencil.

2 LOOK AHEAD

Mass is the amount of matter in an object. One way to find an object's mass is to see how heavy it is. You can use the masses of known objects to estimate other masses. You can use a balance scale to measure mass.

The mass of a paper clip is about 1 **gram**.

The mass of a large hardcover book is about 1 **kilogram**.

a. A wooden baseball bat and a rubber band are shown. Circle the one that has a mass of about 1 gram. Put a box around the one that has a mass of about 1 kilogram.

b. 1 kilogram is the same as 1,000 grams. So, an object with a mass of

1 kilogram is about as heavy as .... paper clips.

3 REFLECT

Elena's brother says the family dog has a mass of 30 grams. Elena says the dog has a mass of 30 kilograms. Who do you think is correct? Why do you think so?

....

....

....

Prepare for Working with Mass

1 Think about what you know about measurement. Fill in each box. Use words, numbers, and pictures. Show as many ideas as you can.

Word	In My Own Words	Example
mass		
gram		
kilogram		

2 A stick of chewing gum and a kitten are shown. Circle the one that has a mass of about 1 gram. Put a box around the one that has a mass of about 1 kilogram.

3 Solve the problem. Show your work.

The paper clip measures about 1 gram on a scale. How could you estimate the mass of the paintbrush? How could you use paper clips to measure the mass of the paintbrush?

Solution

....

....

....

....

....

4 Check your answer. Show your work.

Develop Estimating Mass

Read and try to solve the problem below.

> Jamie bought a medium-sized watermelon at the store.
> Estimate the mass of the watermelon.

TRY IT

 Math Toolkit
- pan balance
- paper clips
- string
- paper plates
- large hardcover books

DISCUSS IT

Ask your partner: Do you agree with me? Why or why not?

Tell your partner: I do not understand how . . .

Explore different ways to understand estimating mass.

> **Jamie bought a medium-sized watermelon at the store.**
> **Estimate the mass of the watermelon.**

PICTURE IT

You can use models to help you estimate the mass of an object.

Jamie picked up the six books shown below. Then he picked up the watermelon. The books and the watermelon seemed to have about the same mass.

MODEL IT

You can use a balance scale to help you estimate or find the mass of an object.

Jamie put the watermelon on one side of the balance scale and some 1-kilogram and 10-gram weights on the other side.

You can see that it takes six 1-kilogram weights and three 10-gram weights to balance the scale. The weights use the abbreviations kg for kilogram and g for gram.

CONNECT IT

Now you will use the problem from the previous page to help you understand how to estimate mass.

1 Look at **Picture It**. Explain why Jamie used books instead of paper clips to help him estimate the mass of the watermelon.

2 The mass of each book is about 1 kilogram. Estimate the mass of the watermelon. Explain how you did it.

3 Look at the balance scale in **Model It**. The two sides of the scale are balanced, so it shows the actual mass of the watermelon. What is the actual mass of the watermelon?

Is the estimate you made in problem 2 close to the actual mass?

4 Explain how you could estimate the mass of a plastic fork.

5 REFLECT

Look back at your **Try It**, strategies by classmates, and **Picture It** and **Model It**. Which models or strategies do you like best for estimating mass? Explain.

....

....

....

....

APPLY IT

Use what you just learned to solve these problems.

6 Would you estimate the mass of a table using grams or kilograms?
Show your work.

Solution ....

7 The scale is being used to measure the mass
of 3 bricks. Estimate the mass of 1 brick.
Show your work.

Solution ....

8 Estimate the mass of a pair of scissors.

Ⓐ 28 grams

Ⓑ 28 kilograms

Ⓒ 2 grams

Ⓓ 2 kilograms

Practice Estimating Mass

**Study the Example showing one way to estimate mass.
Then solve problems 1–8.**

EXAMPLE

Dana wants to estimate how heavy her backpack is when she fills it with hardcover library books.

Each book has a mass of about 1 kilogram.
She can fit 8 books in her backpack.

Dana estimates that her full backpack has a mass of about 9 kilograms, because the backpack has mass too.

1 Would you use grams or kilograms as the unit to measure the mass of a strawberry?

2 Would you use grams or kilograms as the unit to measure the mass of a puppy?

3 Would you use grams or kilograms as the unit to measure the mass of a pen?

4 A 1-liter bottle of water has a mass of about 1 kilogram. Which objects could have a mass of more than 1 kilogram?

Ⓐ a slice of bread　　　　Ⓑ a chair

Ⓒ a watermelon　　　　　Ⓓ a paper bag

Ⓔ a rabbit　　　　　　　Ⓕ a pair of eyeglasses

5 A paper clip has a mass of 1 gram. Estimate the mass of a slice of bread and explain how you figured it out.

Estimated mass:

6 A bottle of water has a mass of 1 kilogram. Estimate the mass of a cat, and explain how you figured it out.

Estimated mass:

7 George says that his bicycle has a mass of 15 grams. Janet says the bicycle has a mass of 15 kilograms. Who do you think is correct? Why do you think so?

8 George takes the front wheel off the bicycle in problem 7 and finds its mass. What could the mass of the wheel be? Explain your reasoning.

Develop Solving Word Problems About Mass

Read and try to solve the problem below.

> **Nick has an orange that has a mass of 220 grams and an apple that has a mass of 110 grams. What is the mass of the orange and apple together?**

TRY IT

 Math Toolkit
- base-ten blocks
- pan balance
- hundreds place-value charts
- 1-centimeter grid paper
- sticky notes

DISCUSS IT

Ask your partner: How did you get started?

Tell your partner: At first, I thought . . .

Explore different ways to understand solving word problems about mass.

> **Nick has an orange that has a mass of 220 grams and an apple that has a mass of 110 grams. What is the mass of the orange and apple together?**

PICTURE IT

You can use a balance scale to help you solve the problem.

The balance scale below shows the mass of the orange.

The balance scale below shows the mass of the apple.

The balance scale below shows the mass of the orange and apple altogether. The orange and apple are on one side of the scale, and the weights are on the other side.

CONNECT IT

Now you will use the problem from the previous page to help you understand how to solve word problems about mass.

1 How do you decide which operation to use to solve this problem?

2 Look at the balance scale in **Picture It** that shows the orange and apple together. What does the picture show that could help you solve the problem?

3 Write an equation for the problem. What is the mass of the orange and apple together?

4 Explain how you could estimate to know that your answer makes sense.

5 Explain why the label *grams* should be part of your answer to this problem.

6 REFLECT

Look back at your **Try It**, strategies by classmates, and **Picture It**. Which models or strategies do you like best for solving word problems about mass? Explain.

....

....

....

....

APPLY IT

Use what you just learned to solve these problems.

7 Jeff has 40 grams of birdseed. He shares it equally among 4 birds.
How many grams of birdseed does each bird get? Show your work.

Solution ....

8 Micah owns two horses. One horse has a mass of 493 kilograms and the
other has a mass of 381 kilograms. What is the difference in mass
between his two horses? Show your work.

Solution ....

9 Jasmine has 30 nickels. Each nickel has a mass of 5 grams. What is the
total mass of Jasmine's nickels? Show your work.

Solution ....

Practice Solving Word Problems About Mass

Study the Example showing how to solve a word problem about mass. Then solve problems 1–7.

EXAMPLE

A tree house is strong enough to hold up to 300 kilograms safely. Can 8 children, each with a mass of about 30 kilograms, be in the tree house at the same time?

$$8 \times 30 = 8 \times 3 \times 10$$
$$= 24 \times 10$$
$$= 240$$

The 8 children have a total mass of about 240 kilograms. 240 kilograms is less than 300 kilograms.

All 8 children can be in the tree house at the same time.

1 Jon has a bag of marbles with a mass of 200 grams. Mark has a bag of marbles with a mass of 215 grams. What is the mass of the two bags of marbles combined?

   The combined mass is ....

2 Brenda has two dogs. Their masses are 27 kilograms and 33 kilograms. What is the mass of the two dogs combined?

   The combined mass is ....

3 Joe is shoveling snow. He estimates that he lifts 3 kilograms of snow with each full shovel. What is the total mass he lifts with 80 full shovels?

   The total mass is about ....

4   A houseplant has a mass of 15 kilograms. Barbara buys 3 houseplants of exactly the same mass. What is the mass of all the houseplants combined? Write an equation to solve the problem. Show your work.

Solution ....

5   Kara's filled lunchbox is 815 grams. Ben's filled lunchbox is 900 grams. How much lighter is Kara's lunchbox? Show your work.

Solution ....

6   Mark has 8 packs of pretzels in a paper bag. Each pack of pretzels is 90 grams. The bag is 85 grams. What is the mass of the paper bag with the pretzels in it? Show your work.

Solution ....

7   Kathy's cloth grocery sack can hold 16 kilograms without ripping. She buys juice, soup, and rice at the store. The table shows the mass for 1 of each item. What is one way she can fill the sack with these items? Show your work.

Item	Mass
juice	2 kilograms
soup	1 kilogram
bag of rice	5 kilograms

Solution ....

Refine Understanding of Mass

Complete the Example below. Then solve problems 1–8.

EXAMPLE

Max has a soccer ball with a mass of 445 grams and a baseball with a mass of 142 grams. What is the difference in mass between the balls?

Look at how you could show your work using an equation.

$$445 - 142 = 303$$

Solution ....

The student wrote a subtraction equation to find the difference in mass.

PAIR/SHARE
How else could you solve this problem?

APPLY IT

1. Ruby's mom buys 4 bags of potatoes. Each bag has a mass of 4 kilograms. What is the total mass of the 4 bags? Show your work.

There are 4 bags with 4 kilograms of potatoes in each bag. That reminds me of using equal groups.

PAIR/SHARE
How did you decide which operation to use to solve the problem?

Solution ....

2 Jane has a sandwich and a banana for lunch. The sandwich's mass is 140 grams. The banana's mass is 130 grams. What is the total mass of the sandwich and the banana? Show your work.

Do not forget to label your answer. Are you finding the total mass in grams or kilograms?

Solution ....

PAIR/SHARE
What question could you ask that would be solved with a subtraction equation?

3 Brock's dad buys a 10-kilogram bag of rice. Then he divides the rice evenly into 5 smaller bags. How many kilograms of rice does each smaller bag have in it?

Will the amount in each smaller bag be greater than or less than 10 kilograms?

Ⓐ 2 kilograms

Ⓑ 5 kilograms

Ⓒ 15 kilograms

Ⓓ 50 kilograms

Felicia chose Ⓓ as the correct answer. How did she get that answer?

PAIR/SHARE
Does Felicia's answer make sense?

4 Which is the best estimate for the mass of a watermelon?

Ⓐ 30 kilograms

Ⓑ 3 kilograms

Ⓒ 30 grams

Ⓓ 3 grams

5 Which objects have a mass of about 1 gram?

Ⓐ rubber band

Ⓑ box of crayons

Ⓒ pair of scissors

Ⓓ dollar bill

Ⓔ library book

6 Mrs. Martin's partly filled shopping bag has a mass of 4 kilograms. Then she adds some potatoes to her bag. The scale shows the mass of the potatoes. What is the mass of the bag, in kilograms, after adding the potatoes?

7 Margo's soccer coach brings a box of small watermelons to practice. The mass of the box with all the watermelons in it is 12 kilograms.

Estimate the number of watermelons in the box. Show your work and explain what you did at each step.

There are about .... watermelons in the box.

8 MATH JOURNAL

Write a word problem about mass that you can solve by using addition or subtraction. Explain how to find the answer.

 SELF CHECK Go back to the Unit 5 Opener and see what you can check off.

Self Reflection

In this unit you learned to . . .

Skill	Lesson
Tell and write time to the nearest minute on digital clocks and clocks with hands and solve problems about time.	27
Estimate liquid volume and solve problems about liquid volume.	28
Estimate mass and solve problems about mass.	29

Think about what you learned.

Use words, numbers, and drawings.

1 Three examples of what I learned are . . .

2 A mistake that helped me learn was . . .

3 One thing I am still confused about is . . .

Solve Measurement Problems

Study an Example Problem and Solution

SMP 1 Make sense of problems and persevere in solving them.

Read this problem involving measurements. Then look at Max's solution to this problem.

Max's Snacks

Max has his laptop and binder in his backpack. He also wants to pack lots of snacks. He can pack snacks with a mass of up to 1,000 grams. That way, the backpack isn't too heavy.

Snack Choices

orange – 95 g   box of crackers – 338 g

bag of cookies – 424 g   apple – 142 g

granola bar – 22 g   bag of almonds – 42 g

banana – 124 g   peanut butter – 345 g

giant sandwich – 365 g

Choose snack items Max can pack. You may use an item more than once. Give the total mass of the snacks. Show that your solution works.

Read the sample solution on the next page. Then look at the checklist below. Find and mark parts of the solution that match the checklist.

✓ PROBLEM-SOLVING CHECKLIST

☐ Tell what is known.

☐ Tell what the problem is asking.

☐ Show all your work.

☐ Show that the solution works.

a. **Circle** something that is known.

b. **Underline** something that you need to find.

c. **Draw a box around** what you do to solve the problem.

d. **Put a checkmark** next to the part that shows the solution works.

MAX'S SOLUTION

Hi, I'm Max. Here's how I solved this problem.

- **I know the mass of each snack.**

  I will pick my favorite snacks and add the masses.

- **I really want my giant sandwich and an apple.**

  $$\begin{array}{r} 365 \\ +142 \\ \hline 7 \\ 100 \\ +400 \\ \hline 507 \end{array}$$ sandwich apple

  I can still add about 500 more grams of food.

  507 is about 500 and 500 + 500 is 1,000.

- **I love peanut butter and bananas.**

  $$\begin{array}{r} 345 \\ +124 \\ \hline 469 \end{array}$$ peanut butter banana

- **I can add to see what the total is for all 4 items.**

  $$\begin{array}{r} 507 \\ +469 \\ \hline 16 \\ 60 \\ +900 \\ \hline 976 \end{array}$$

- **Add up to see how much is left.**

  976 + 4 is 980 and 20 more is 1,000.

  So, I have 24 grams left.

- **It looks like I still have room for a granola bar.**

  $$\begin{array}{r} 976 \\ +\ \ 22 \\ \hline 998 \end{array}$$ granola bar

  I like that I got so close to 1,000 grams.

- **The total is 2 grams less than 1,000.**

  I can not pack anything else. I'll pack a giant sandwich, an apple, a banana, peanut butter, and a granola bar.

Try Another Approach

There are many ways to solve problems. Think about how you might solve Max's Snacks problem in a different way.

Max's Snacks

Max has his laptop and binder in his backpack. He also wants to pack lots of snacks. He can pack snacks with a mass of up to 1,000 grams. That way, the backpack isn't too heavy.

Snack Choices

orange – 95 g	box of crackers – 338 g
bag of cookies – 424 g	apple – 142 g
granola bar – 22 g	bag of almonds – 42 g
banana – 124 g	peanut butter – 345 g
giant sandwich – 365 g	

Choose snack items Max can pack. You may use an item more than once. Give the total mass of the snacks. Show that your solution works.

PLAN IT

Answer these questions to help you start thinking about a plan.

A. Could you solve the problem by starting with 1,000 grams? Explain.

B. Do you want a lot of lighter snacks or a few heavier snacks?

SOLVE IT

Find a different solution for Max's Snacks problem. Show all your work on a separate sheet of paper.

You may want to use the Problem-Solving Tips to get started.

PROBLEM-SOLVING TIPS

● **Models**

● **Word Bank**

| add | sum | mass |
| subtract | difference | grams |

● **Sentence Starters**

• I can start with _____

• I want to pack _____

REFLECT

Use Mathematical Practices Choose one of these questions to discuss with a partner.

• **Reason Mathematically** What strategies can you use to add or subtract?

• **Persevere** What are some different ways that you could start your solution?

Discuss Models and Strategies

Read the problem. Write a solution on a separate sheet of paper.
Remember, there can be lots of ways to solve a problem!

Max's Snack Bars

Max is making his favorite snack bars. He will share them with friends. He does not remember the exact amount of each ingredient. He writes down what he does remember.

Nut and Honey Snack Bars

Ingredients

Honey and Oat cereal

peanuts

raisins

peanut butter

honey

Snack Bar Notes

- The ingredients are all measured in grams.
- The ingredient with the greatest mass is peanuts.
- Use less than 50 grams of cereal.
- Use less than 100 grams of peanut butter.
- The amount of peanut butter is about double the amount of honey.
- The total mass of all ingredients is about 500 grams.

How much of each ingredient should Max use in his snack bars?

PLAN IT AND SOLVE IT

Find a solution for Max's Snack Bars problem.

Write a recipe for Max's Snack Bars. Be sure to include:

• the amount of each ingredient to use.

• how you decided each amount.

• the total mass of snack bars Max will make.

You may want to use the Problem-Solving Tips to get started.

PROBLEM-SOLVING TIPS

● **Questions**

  • How could you use estimation in your solution?

  • What numbers could you use that are easy to work with?

● **Sentence Starters**

• I can start with _____

• The mass of the peanuts _____

☑ **PROBLEM-SOLVING CHECKLIST**

Make sure that you . . .

☐ tell what you know.

☐ tell what you need to do.

☐ show all your work.

☐ show that the solution works.

REFLECT

Use Mathematical Practices Choose one of these questions to discuss with a partner.

• **Make Sense of Problems** How is this like other problems you have solved in this lesson? How is it different?

• **Make an Argument** How can you be sure that your solution works with all the information Max wrote down?

Unit 5 Math in Action Solve Measurement Problems

Persevere On Your Own

Read the problem. Write a solution on a separate sheet of paper.

Soup Snacks

Max plans to make tomato soup. His recipe makes 24 liters of soup. He will freeze the soup in containers. Then he'll have plenty of soup snacks ready to go.

Max wants to buy some 1-liter containers for the soup. He can buy different packages of 1-liter containers.

- package of 4 containers
- package of 5 containers
- package of 6 containers

What packages should Max buy?

SOLVE IT

Tell Max what packages to buy.

- Tell how many containers Max needs.

- Tell which packages Max should buy.

- Tell how many of each package he should buy.

- Show why your solution gives the exact number of containers Max needs.

REFLECT

Use Mathematical Practices Choose one of these questions to discuss with a partner.

- **Reason Mathematically** How can you tell by looking at the numbers if a package will work or not?

- **Use Models** How did you use basic facts to find a solution?

Chore List

Max has a busy Saturday. He makes a list of chores he needs to do and how many minutes the chore will take.

He leaves for a basketball game at 2:22 PM.

Max wants to do at least two chores before he leaves for the game.

He starts his chores at 1:33 PM.

Chore List

Clean my room	15 min
Do homework	35 min
Help Mom	25 min
Wash dishes	10 min

Which chores could Max do before he leaves for the basketball game?

SOLVE IT

Help Max decide which chores to do before the game.

• Tell which chores Max can do before the game.

• Explain your choices.

• Show why your solution works.

REFLECT

Use Mathematical Practices After you complete the task, choose one of these questions to discuss with a partner.

• **Use Models** What models did you use?

• **Reason with Numbers** How could an estimate help you begin this problem?

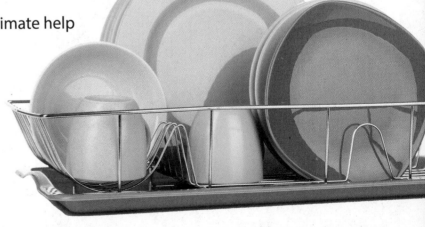

Unit Review

1 Mr. Jones makes 19 liters of punch for a party. He needs 36 liters of punch. How many more liters of punch does he need to make for the party? Show your work.

Solution ....

2 Decide if each container can hold more than 3 liters. Choose *Yes* or *No* for each container.

	Yes	**No**
tea cup	Ⓐ	Ⓑ
shampoo bottle	Ⓒ	Ⓓ
bathtub	Ⓔ	Ⓕ
fish aquarium	Ⓖ	Ⓗ
juice box	Ⓘ	Ⓙ

3 Angelica leaves home at 7:48 AM. It takes her 27 minutes to get to school. What time does Angelica arrive at school?

Ⓐ 8:27 AM

Ⓑ 8:21 AM

Ⓒ 8:15 AM

Ⓓ 8:08 AM

4 Would you estimate the mass of a plastic cup using grams or kilograms? Explain why you chose your answer.

....

....

....

....

Solution ....

5 Danielle works at a bakery. She needs to separate 42 kilograms of flour into each of 6 smaller containers. If she separates the flour into equal amounts, how many kilograms of flour will she put in each container? Show your work.

Solution ....

6 The clock shows the time that Ken eats dinner.

What time does Ken eat dinner? Explain your answer.

....

....

....

....

Performance Task

Answer the question and show all your work on separate paper.

Darian delivers supplies to aquariums. Darian has 3 deliveries to make tomorrow. She can make only 2 deliveries before returning to the store to pick up more supplies. She wants to finish all three deliveries and be back at the store by 3 PM.

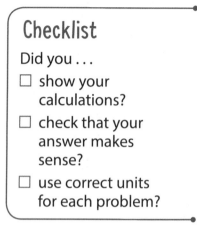

- A delivery to Fish Zoo takes 35 minutes.

- A delivery to Submarine World takes 40 minutes.

- A delivery to Under the Sea takes 1 hour.

- Picking up more supplies at the store takes 10 minutes.

The times above do not include travel time. Below is a map that shows the time it takes Darian to drive between the locations.

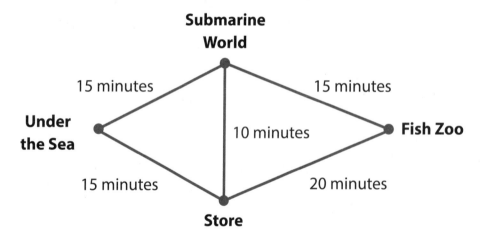

Describe or show one route that Darian can take to make all three deliveries. What is the latest time Darian should start making deliveries so she can finish and get back to the store by 3 PM?

REFLECT

Use Mathematical Practices After you complete the task, choose one of following questions to answer.

- **Reason Mathematically** What information did you need to find before deciding on a route?

- **Use Tools** How can a clock be used to find the time when Darian finished each delivery?

Vocabulary

Draw or write to show examples for each term. Then draw or write to show other math words in the unit.

elapsed time the amount of time that has passed between a start time and an end time.

My Example

gram (g) a unit of mass in the metric system. A paper clip has a mass of about 1 gram. There are 1,000 grams in 1 kilogram.

My Example

kilogram (kg) a unit of mass in the metric system. There are 1,000 grams in 1 kilogram.

My Example

liquid volume the amount of space a liquid takes up.

My Example

liter (L) a unit of liquid volume in the metric system. There are 1,000 milliliters in 1 liter.

My Example

mass the amount of matter in an object. Measuring the mass of an object is one way to measure how heavy it is. Units of mass include the gram and kilogram.

My Example

minute (min)   a unit of time. There are 60 minutes in 1 hour and 60 seconds in 1 minute.

My Example

My Word: _____

_____

_____

My Example

My Word: _____

_____

_____

My Example

My Word: _____

_____

_____

My Example

My Word: _____

_____

_____

My Example

My Word: _____

_____

_____

My Example

☑ SELF CHECK

Before starting this unit, check off the skills you know below. As you complete each lesson, see how many more skills you can check off!

I can . . .	Before	After
Describe shapes, compare them, and put them in groups that tell how they are alike, for example: by the number of sides or by whether they have right angles.	☐	☐
Compare quadrilaterals and put them in groups based on their attributes, for example: all 4 sides are the same length or there are 2 pairs of parallel sides.	☐	☐
Solve problems involving perimeters, including finding an unknown side length, and finding rectangles with the same perimeter and different areas, or with the same area and different perimeters.	☐	☐
Divide rectangles into parts with equal area and name the area of shaded parts using unit fractions.	☐	☐

Build Your Vocabulary

Math Vocabulary

Work with a small group to complete the table. Match the review word to the shape in the first column. Then work together to complete the table.

Shape	Name	Description

Academic Vocabulary

Put a check next to the academic words you know. Then use the words to complete the sentences.

☐ in common   ☐ describe   ☐ classify   ☐ identify

1 When I .... a triangle, I say it has three sides and three angles.

2 A quadrilateral and a rhombus have something .... : they both have four sides.

3 We are learning how to .... plants based on their characteristics.

4 I can .... a hexagon by counting the number of sides and angles.

Understand Categories of Shapes

Dear Family,

This week your child is exploring how shapes can be named and grouped according to their features.

A **rectangle** is any quadrilateral with 4 right angles.

A **rhombus** is any quadrilateral with 4 sides that are all the same length.

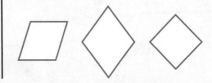

The tables below show one way to sort shapes based on a few of their features. The left side of the top table shows shapes that have 4 right angles. The right side of the top table shows shapes that have 4 sides all the same length. The bottom table shows you the shapes that have both 4 right angles *and* 4 sides all the same length. This bottom table tells you that a square is both a rectangle and a rhombus.

4 right angles	4 sides all the same length
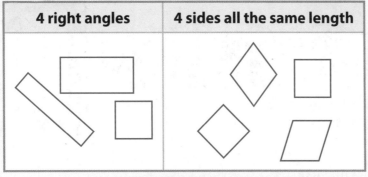	

4 right angles *and* 4 sides all the same length
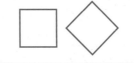

Invite your child to share what he or she knows about shapes by doing the following activity together.

ACTIVITY   DESCRIBING SHAPES

Do this activity with your child to understand categories of shapes.

Support your child as he or she learns to recognize the features of different shapes by doing this activity together.

Be on the lookout for flat shapes around your home such as mirrors, rugs, tiles, and so forth. As a starting point, look at the shapes in the pictures below.

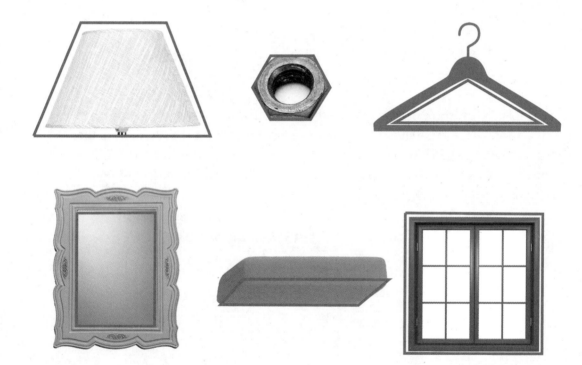

Take turns describing the shapes. For each shape, describe:
- the number of sides.
- the lengths of the sides.
- the lengths of opposite sides.
- the number of angles.
- the number of right angles.

Then pick two shapes. How are they alike? How are they different?

Now look at other shapes around your house, and have similar discussions about how they are alike and different.

Explore Categories of Shapes

How do sides and angles help you name and group shapes?

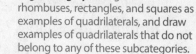
MODEL IT

Complete the problems below.

1 One way to name shapes or to group shapes that are alike in some way is by the number of sides. For example, this shape has 3 sides.

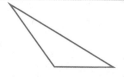

Write the name of this shape. ....

2 Another way to group shapes is by the lengths of their sides. You can use a ruler to measure the sides of the shapes.

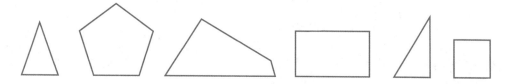

a. Write *N* on the shapes above with no sides the same length.

b. Write *S* on the shapes above with some sides the same length.

c. Write *A* on the shapes above with all sides the same length.

3 Opposite sides in a quadrilateral do not touch. Circle the shapes below that have opposite sides the same length.

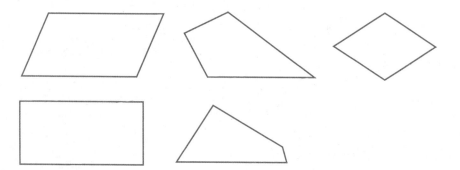

DISCUSS IT

- Did you and your partner have the same answers for problem 2?

- I think the sides of a shape can help you name and group shapes because . . .

MODEL IT

Complete the problems below.

4 You can also use the number and type of angles or corners to name and group shapes. Angles that look like the corners of a square are called **right angles**. Shapes can have no right angles, some right angles, or all right angles.

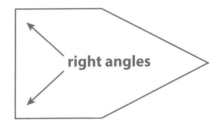

a. Tell how many angles each shape below has.

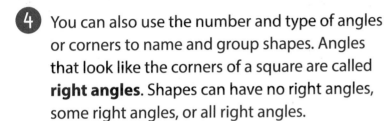

. . . .

b. Tell how many right angles each shape below has.

. . . .

5 REFLECT

What are some ways you can name or group shapes?

. . . .

. . . .

. . . .

DISCUSS IT

• Did you have trouble deciding which angles were right angles?

• I think using angles to name and group shapes is like using sides because . . .

Prepare for Exploring Categories of Shapes

1 Think about what you know about shapes. Fill in each box. Use words, numbers, and pictures. Show as many ideas as you can.

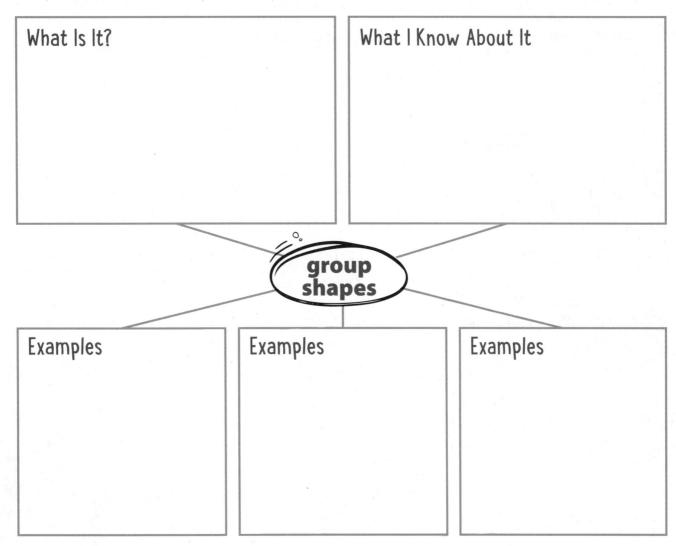

What Is It?	What I Know About It

group shapes

Examples	Examples	Examples

2 You can use opposite sides to group shapes. In the shapes below, the opposite sides are the sides that do not touch. Circle the shapes that appear to have opposite sides the same length.

Solve.

3 One way to name or group shapes is by the number of sides. For example, this shape has 4 sides.

Write the name of this shape. ....

4 Another way to group shapes is by the lengths of their sides. You can use a ruler to measure the sides of the shapes.

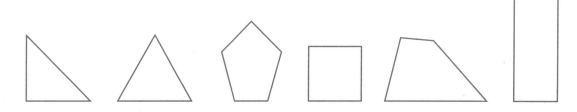

a. Write *N* on the shapes above with no sides the same length.

b. Write *S* on the shapes above with some sides the same length.

c. Write *A* on the shapes above with all sides the same length.

5 You can also use the number and type of angles to name and group shapes. Shapes can have no right angles, some right angles, or all right angles.

Tell how many right angles each shape below has.

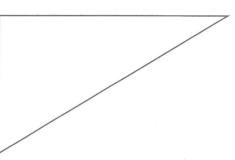

....

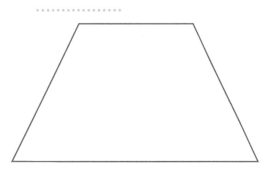

....

Develop Understanding of Comparing Shapes

MODEL IT: SORT SHAPES

Use the shapes below for problems 1 and 2.

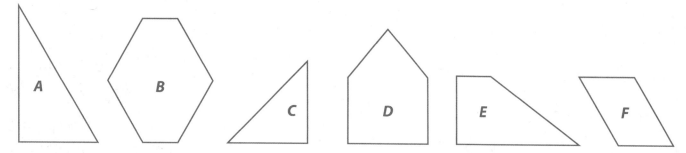

1. Look at the sides and angles of the shapes to sort them into the groups below. Write the letter of each shape in the correct column. Some shapes may belong in both groups.

Some right angles	Some sides the same length

2. Use your answer to problem 1 to choose the shapes that belong in the group below.

Some right angles *and* some sides the same length

DISCUSS IT

- Did you and your partner choose the same shapes for each group?

- I think the group in problem 2 is like the two groups in problem 1 because . . .

MODEL IT: DESCRIBE SHAPES

Complete the following problem.

3 Describe the sides and angles of each triangle below in as many ways as you can.

a.

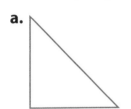

b.

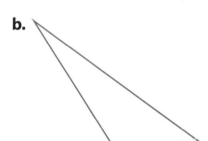

> ## DISCUSS IT
>
> • Did you and your partner come up with the same descriptions in problem 3?
>
> • I think describing shapes is like sorting shapes because . . .

CONNECT IT

Complete the problems below.

4 How did sorting shapes in problems 1 and 2 on the previous page help you describe the triangles in problem 3 above?

5 Describe two groups that both triangles in problem 3 belong to.

Practice Comparing Shapes

Study how the Example shows comparing shapes by the number of right angles and the lengths of sides. Then solve problems 1–6.

EXAMPLE

Which shapes have at least one right angle?

A right angle is an angle that looks like the corner of a square.

The square and rectangle have 4 right angles each.

Triangle F has 1 right angle.

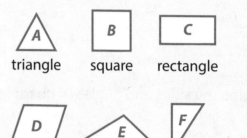

Use the shapes above to answer problems 1 and 2.

1   Sort the shapes above into the groups below. Write the letter of each shape in the correct column.

All sides the same length	Only some sides the same length	All sides are different lengths

2   Do all the triangles above have right angles? Explain.

Use the two quadrilaterals below for problems 3–5.

3 Describe the sides and angles of quadrilateral A in as many ways as you can.

4 Describe the sides and angles of quadrilateral B in as many ways as you can.

5 Describe two groups that both quadrilaterals belong to.

6 Write the name of two different groups that each shape below belongs to.

a.

b.

Refine Ideas About Comparing Shapes

APPLY IT

Complete these problems on your own.

① COMPARE

Think about how these shapes are alike and different. You can use a ruler to measure the sides.

Write two ways in which these shapes are alike.

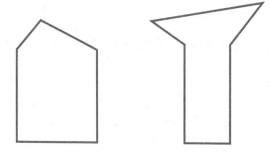

Write two ways in which these shapes are different.

② EXPLAIN

Gwen says that all rectangles belong in the group *some right angles*. Li says that all rectangles belong in the group *all right angles*. Who is correct? Explain.

③ ILLUSTRATE

Draw a shape that belongs to both of these groups: *all sides are the same length* and *no right angles*.

PAIR/SHARE
Discuss your solutions for these three problems with a partner.

Use what you have learned to complete problem 4.

4 Think about the ways you grouped shapes in this lesson.

Part A Think of two different ways you can put shapes into groups. Describe each group on the lines below.

Group 1: ....

Group 2: ....

Draw one shape that belongs to one group but not the other.

Tell which group the shape belongs to. Then explain why it does not belong to the other group.

Part B Draw a shape that belongs to both groups in Part A, or explain why there is no shape that belongs to both groups.

5 MATH JOURNAL

Name a group that shape A belongs to but shape B does not. Next, name a group that shape B belongs to but shape A does not. Then name a group that both shapes belong to.

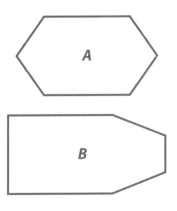

Classify Quadrilaterals

Dear Family,

This week your child is learning to classify quadrilaterals.

A quadrilateral is any flat shape with 4 sides and 4 angles. You can use **attributes** or features to describe a shape, like number of sides, or lengths of sides.

Parallelograms, rectangles, and rhombuses are all examples of quadrilaterals. A **parallelogram** is a quadrilateral where opposite sides are parallel and equal in length. All rectangles and rhombuses are parallelograms.

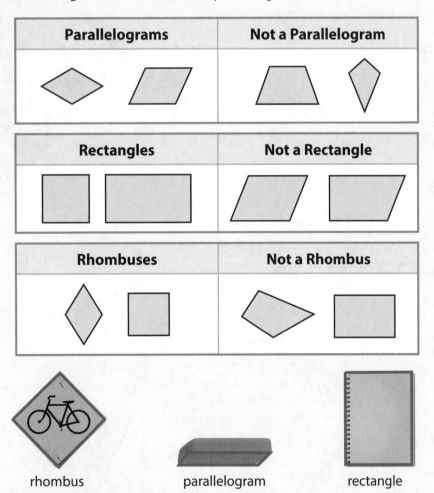

Parallelograms	Not a Parallelogram

Rectangles	Not a Rectangle

Rhombuses	Not a Rhombus

rhombus   parallelogram   rectangle

Invite your child to share what he or she knows about classifying quadrilaterals by doing the following activity together.

ACTIVITY CLASSIFYING QUADRILATERALS

Do this activity with your child to explore classifying quadrilaterals.

Materials 8 different writing tools such as pens, pencils, markers, crayons
(4 should be the same length)

Invite your child to create a quadrilateral using 4 of the writing tools
as the sides of the shape. You create a quadrilateral with the other 4.
See below for an example.

Together, describe your quadrilaterals. For example:

- Tell the number of right angles.

- Find any opposite sides that are the same length.

Now classify both of your quadrilaterals. Is your quadrilateral:

- a rectangle?   Yes   No

- a square?   Yes   No

- a rhombus?   Yes   No

- a parallelogram?   Yes   No

- none of the above?   Yes   No

If your quadrilateral is none of the above, see if you can figure out what you
would need to change in your shape to make it fit at least one of the
classifications listed. Try it to check your thinking!

©Curriculum Associates, LLC   Copying is not permitted.

Explore Classifying Quadrilaterals

Previously you compared shapes and put them into groups. In this lesson you will learn how to group quadrilaterals. Use what you know to try to solve the problem below.

A rhombus is one kind of quadrilateral. A rectangle is another kind of quadrilateral. How are a rhombus and a rectangle the same? How are they different?

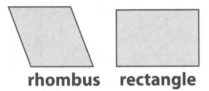

rhombus   **rectangle**

Learning Target

- Understand that shapes in different categories may share attributes, and that the shared attributes can define a larger category. Recognize rhombuses, rectangles, and squares as examples of quadrilaterals, and draw examples of quadrilaterals that do not belong to any of these subcategories.

SMP 1, 2, 3, 4, 5, 6, 7

TRY IT

 Math Toolkit
- geoboards
- rubber bands
- grid paper
- index cards
- sticky notes

DISCUSS IT

Ask your partner: Can you explain that again?

Tell your partner: I knew . . . so I . . .

CONNECT IT

❶ LOOK BACK

How are a rhombus and a rectangle alike? How are they different?

❷ LOOK AHEAD

A quadrilateral is a shape with 4 sides and 4 angles.
The shapes to the right are quadrilaterals. You can
name a quadrilateral based on its attributes.
An **attribute** is a way to describe a shape.

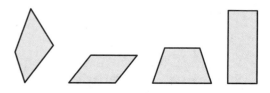

a. A quadrilateral is a **parallelogram** if it has the attributes *both pairs of*
opposite sides are the same length and *opposites sides are parallel.*
Sides are **parallel** if they are always the same distance apart.

Circle the parallelograms:

b. A quadrilateral is a rectangle if it has 4 right angles. A rectangle also has
2 pairs of opposite sides that are parallel and the same length.

Circle the rectangles:

c. A quadrilateral is a rhombus if it has 4 sides that are all the same length.
A rhombus also has 2 pairs of parallel sides.

Circle the rhombuses:

❸ REFLECT

List 3 attributes a quadrilateral could have.

....

....

Prepare for Classifying Quadrilaterals

1 Think about what you know about quadrilaterals. Fill in each box. Use words, numbers, and pictures. Show as many ideas as you can.

Word	In My Own Words	Example
quadrilateral		
attribute		
parallelogram		
rectangle		
rhombus		

2 Circle the parallelograms. What other word above describes your circled shapes?

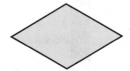  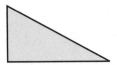

3 Solve the problem. Show your work.

A parallelogram is one kind of quadrilateral. A square is another kind of quadrilateral. How are a parallelogram and a square the same? How are they different?

parallelogram   square

Solution

4 Check your answer. Show your work.

Develop Comparing Quadrilaterals

Read and try to solve the problem below.

> **Is a square a rectangle?**
>
> **Is a rectangle a square?**

TRY IT

 Math Toolkit
- geoboards
- rubber bands
- grid paper
- dot paper
- colored pencils

DISCUSS IT

Ask your partner: Do you agree with me? Why or why not?

Tell your partner: I agree with you about . . . because . . .

Explore different ways to understand comparing quadrilaterals.

Is a square a rectangle?

Is a rectangle a square?

PICTURE IT

You can use a drawing to compare quadrilaterals.

All quadrilaterals have 4 sides and 4 angles.

4 right angles
2 pairs of parallel sides
4 sides the same length

4 right angles
2 pairs of parallel sides
2 pairs of opposite sides the same length

MODEL IT

You can use a table to compare quadrilaterals.

Shape	4 sides 4 angles	4 right angles	2 pairs of parallel sides	2 pairs of opposite sides that are the same length	4 sides that are the same length
Square	✓	✓	✓	✓	✓
Rectangle	✓	✓	✓	✓	sometimes

CONNECT IT

Now you will use the problem from the previous page to help you understand how to compare quadrilaterals.

1 What is an attribute of a square that is not an attribute of every rectangle?

2 Does every rectangle have all the attributes of a square? ....

3 Does every square have all the attributes of a rectangle? ....

4 Is every square a rectangle? Explain why or why not.

5 Is every rectangle a square? Explain why or why not.

6 REFLECT

Look back at your **Try It**, strategies by classmates, and **Picture It** and **Model It**. Which models or strategies do you like best for comparing quadrilaterals? Explain.

....

....

....

....

....

APPLY IT

Use what you just learned to solve these problems.

7 Circle all the quadrilaterals below that are squares.

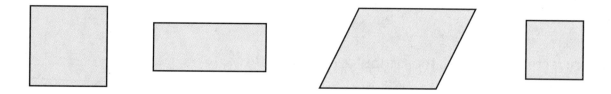

8 One way to define a trapezoid is a quadrilateral with exactly one pair of parallel sides. Draw a trapezoid with two right angles.

9 Circle all the quadrilaterals below that are rectangles.

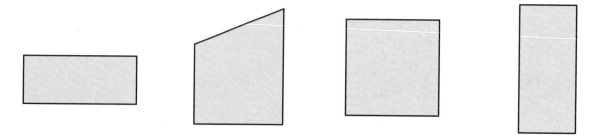

Practice Comparing Quadrilaterals

**Study the Example showing how to compare quadrilaterals.
Then solve problems 1–7.**

EXAMPLE

Which of these shapes are parallelograms?

You can list the attributes of a parallelogram in a table.
Check if each shape always has these attributes.

Attribute	Trapezoid	Rhombus	Rectangle
4 sides	yes	yes	yes
4 angles	yes	yes	yes
2 pairs of parallel sides	no	yes	yes
2 pairs of sides that are the same length	no	yes	yes

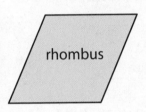

trapezoid

rhombus

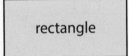

rectangle

A rhombus and a rectangle have all the attributes of a parallelogram.

1 Is shape *A* a parallelogram? Explain.

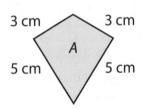

3 cm   3 cm

A

5 cm   5 cm

2 What is another kind of quadrilateral that is also a parallelogram? Explain.

3 Fill in the blanks. Use information from the table above.

Every .... is a parallelogram.

Every .... is a parallelogram.

> **Vocabulary**
>
> **attribute** a way to describe a shape, like number of sides or length of sides.

Use the table to solve problems 4–7.

Attribute	Parallelogram	Rhombus	Rectangle	Square
4 sides and 4 angles	yes	yes	yes	yes
4 right angles	sometimes	sometimes	yes	yes
2 pairs of parallel sides	yes	yes	yes	yes
2 pairs of sides that are the same length	yes	yes	yes	yes

4 Circle all the quadrilaterals that are rhombuses.

5 Circle all the quadrilaterals that are rectangles.

6 Tell whether each sentence is *True* or *False*.

	True	False
All squares are rectangles.	Ⓐ	Ⓑ
All rectangles are parallelograms.	Ⓒ	Ⓓ
All parallelograms are rectangles.	Ⓔ	Ⓕ
All quadrilaterals are parallelograms.	Ⓖ	Ⓗ
All parallelograms are quadrilaterals.	Ⓘ	Ⓙ

7 Jaime says that some rectangles are not squares. Do you agree? Explain.

Develop Naming and Drawing Quadrilaterals

Read and try to solve the problem below.

> **I have a quadrilateral. It has 4 sides that are all the same length. It does not have any right angles. What is the name of my shape?**

TRY IT

 Math Toolkit
- geoboards
- rubber bands
- rulers
- grid paper
- dot paper
- toothpicks

DISCUSS IT

Ask your partner: Do you agree with me? Why or why not?

Tell your partner: I agree with you about . . . because . . .

Explore different ways to understand naming and drawing quadrilaterals.

> **I have a quadrilateral. It has 4 sides that are all the same length. It does not have any right angles. What is the name of my shape?**

MODEL IT

You can make a model to help name a quadrilateral.

Choose 4 toothpicks all the same length. Arrange them to look like a quadrilateral. Make sure there are no right angles.

It does not have any right angles, so it is not a square.

SOLVE IT

You can make a list of the attributes to help you name a quadrilateral.

Look at the model above. Think about everything you know about this shape.

*   It is a quadrilateral, so it has 4 sides and 4 angles.

*   It has 4 sides that are all the same length.

*   It does not have any right angles, so it is not a square.

Using the list of attributes, you can name the shape.

CONNECT IT

Now you will use the problem from the previous page to help you understand how to name and draw quadrilaterals by looking at their attributes.

1 What is the name of the shape described on the previous page? How do you know?

2 Look at the shape to the right. Is it a quadrilateral? Explain why or why not.

3 Is the shape a parallelogram? Is it a rectangle? Is it a rhombus? Explain.

4 Draw a different quadrilateral that is NOT a parallelogram, a rectangle, or a rhombus.

5 REFLECT

Look back at your **Try It**, strategies by classmates, and **Model It** and **Solve It**. Which models or strategies do you like best for naming and drawing quadrilaterals? Explain.

....

....

....

....

APPLY IT

Use what you just learned to solve these problems.

6 Circle all the quadrilaterals below that have 2 pairs of sides the same length, but are not rectangles.

7 Draw a quadrilateral that has at least 1 right angle, but is not a rectangle.

8 Draw a quadrilateral in which all sides are not the same length, opposite sides are the same length, and there are no right angles. Then name the quadrilateral.

Solution ....

Practice Naming and Drawing Quadrilaterals

Study the Example showing how to name a quadrilateral.
Then solve problems 1–9.

EXAMPLE

Justin is drawing a quadrilateral with opposite sides that are the same length. All 4 sides are not the same length. What quadrilaterals can Justin draw?

Make a drawing to see what the quadrilaterals might look like.

 Opposite sides are the same length.
The shape has 4 right angles.

Opposite sides are the same length.
The shape has no right angles.

Justin can draw a rectangle or a parallelogram.

Use the shape on the right to answer problems 1–5.

1 One wall of a shed looks like the shape on the right. How many sides and angles does the shape have?

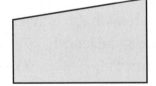

2 How many parallel sides does the shape have?

3 How many right angles does the shape have?

4 Does the shape have 2 pairs of sides the same length?

5 Circle all the words you can use to name this shape.

quadrilateral   parallelogram   rectangle

Use the clues and shapes A–E to solve problems 6–8.

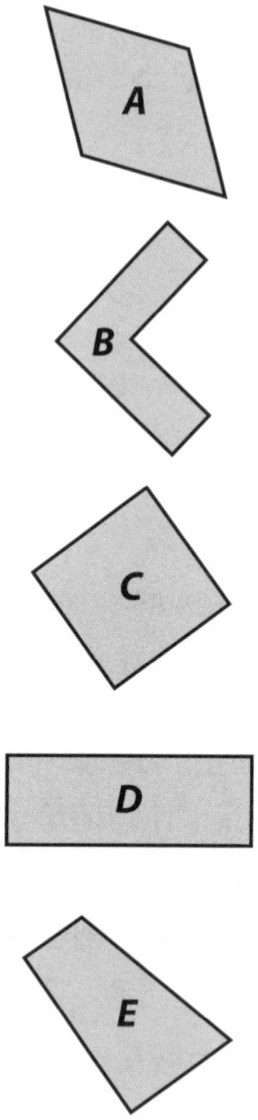

6. I have 4 sides. I am a parallelogram.
   I have all right angles.
   I am not a square.

   I am shape ....

   I am a ....

7. I am a quadrilateral.
   I do not have any right angles.
   My sides are all the same length.

   I am shape ....

   I am a ....

8. I have more than 1 right angle.
   Some of my sides are the same length.
   I am not a quadrilateral.

   I am shape ....

   I am a ....

9. Draw a quadrilateral that has at least 3 right angles, 2 pairs of parallel sides, and all sides the same length. Write all of the possible names for your shape. Tell why the names fit.

A

B

C

D

E

Refine Classifying Quadrilaterals

Complete the Example below. Then solve problems 1–9.

EXAMPLE

A patio has 2 pairs of sides that are the same length. All sides are not the same length, but it does have 4 right angles. What shape is the patio?

Look at how you could show your work using a model.

Solution ....

The student used a geoboard to model the shape. Now you can see what the shape looks like.

PAIR/SHARE
How else could you model the shape?

APPLY IT

1. Draw a quadrilateral that has no sides the same length and no right angles. Show your work.

The shape you draw will not be a rectangle or a square. It will not be a parallelogram or a rhombus.

PAIR/SHARE
What is a different shape you can draw to solve the problem?

2 Friona cut along the dashed line shown on the shape below. She knows that she made two quadrilaterals.

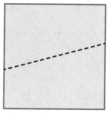

It may help to list the attributes of a parallelogram.

Is either of Friona's quadrilaterals a parallelogram? Explain why or why not.

Solution ....

....

....

PAIR/SHARE
List the attributes of each of Friona's quadrilaterals.

3 Which shape is NOT a rectangle?

What are the attributes of each shape?

Ⓐ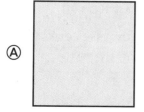

Ⓑ

Ⓒ

Ⓓ

Ari chose Ⓐ as the correct answer. How did he get that answer?

PAIR/SHARE
What are four ways to name the shape Ari chose?

4 A rhombus must have all of these attributes except which one?

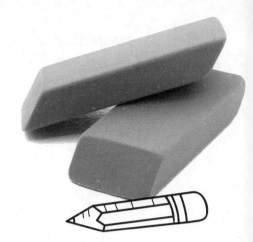

Ⓐ 4 sides that are the same length

Ⓑ 2 pairs of parallel sides

Ⓒ 4 right angles

Ⓓ 4 sides and 4 angles

5 What is the best name that describes all the shapes below? ....

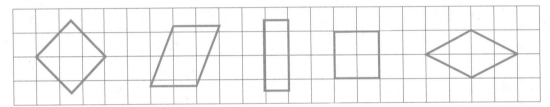

6 Use the grid below. Draw a quadrilateral that belongs to at least two of these groups: *parallelogram*, *rectangle*, or *square*. Explain why your shape belongs to these groups. Show your work.

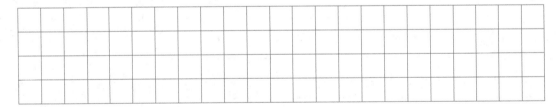

Lesson 31 Classify Quadrilaterals   **707**

7 Use the grid below. Draw a quadrilateral that does NOT belong to any of these groups: *parallelogram*, *rectangle*, or *square*. Explain why your shape does not belong to any of these groups. Show your work.

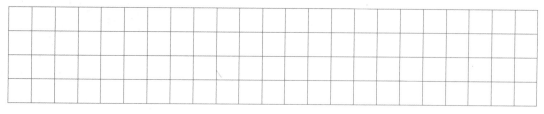

8 Tell whether each sentence is *True* or *False*.

	True	False
All rhombuses are quadrilaterals.	Ⓐ	Ⓑ
All rectangles are squares.	Ⓒ	Ⓓ
All parallelograms are rectangles.	Ⓔ	Ⓕ
All quadrilaterals are parallelograms.	Ⓖ	Ⓗ
All squares are rhombuses.	Ⓘ	Ⓙ

9 MATH JOURNAL

Jess says that a square cannot be a rectangle because a rectangle has 2 long sides and 2 short sides. Is he correct? Explain.

✓ SELF CHECK Go back to the Unit 6 Opener and see what you can check off.

Area and Perimeter of Shapes

Dear Family,

This week your child is learning about perimeter and how it relates to area.

Area tells how much space a shape covers. The area of this shape is 8 square centimeters.

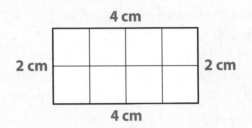

Perimeter tells you the total distance around a shape. You can find the perimeter of a shape by adding the lengths of all the sides:

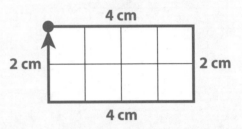

$4 + 2 + 4 + 2 = 12$

The perimeter of this rectangle is 12 centimeters.

Two rectangles can have the same area but different perimeters. For example, this rectangle also has an area of 8 square centimeters, but the perimeter is 18 centimeters.

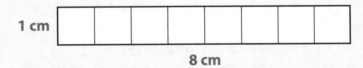

1 cm

8 cm

Also, two rectangles may have different areas, but the same perimeter.

Invite your child to share what he or she knows about area and perimeter by doing the following activity together.

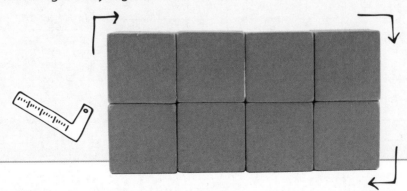

ACTIVITY AREA AND PERIMETER

Do this activity with your child to explore area and perimeter of shapes.

Materials number cube, pencil, grids below

Part 1 Find rectangles with the same area, but different perimeters.
- Roll the number cube.
- Have your child draw a rectangle on the grid below with a length equal to the number on the cube and a width of 4.
- Together, find the area and the perimeter of the rectangle.
- Now, work together to draw another rectangle that has the *same area* but a *different perimeter*. Is there more than one possibility?

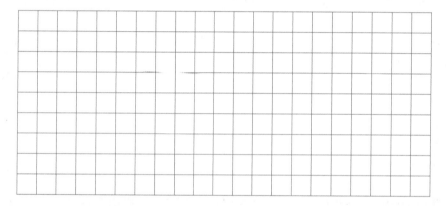

Part 2 Find rectangles with the same perimeter, but different areas.
- Roll the number cube again.
- Again, draw a rectangle on the grid below with a length equal to the number on the cube and a width of 4.
- Together, find the area and the perimeter of the rectangle.
- Now, draw another rectangle that has the *same perimeter* but a *different area*. Is there more than one possibility?

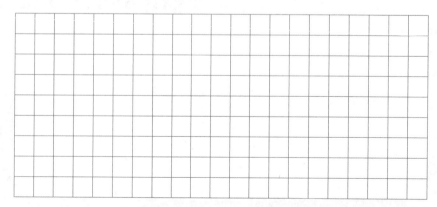

Explore Area and Perimeter of Shapes

In earlier lessons you learned about area. Now you will learn about another measurable attribute of shapes called perimeter. You will also look at how the perimeter of a rectangle is related to its area. Use what you know to try to solve the problem below.

Claire runs along the edges of the soccer field at school. She runs around the whole field one time. How far does Claire run?

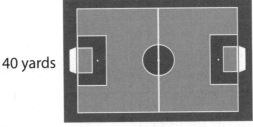

60 yards

40 yards   40 yards

60 yards

TRY IT

Math Toolkit
• base-ten blocks
• grid paper
• number lines
• perimeter and area tool

DISCUSS IT

Ask your partner: How did you get started?

Tell your partner: I started by . . .

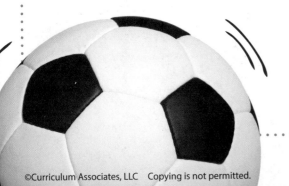

CONNECT IT

① LOOK BACK

How did you find how far Claire runs? Explain.

② LOOK AHEAD

You have already learned about finding area, the amount of space a shape covers. **Perimeter** is the distance around a shape. The red line around the soccer field shows its perimeter.

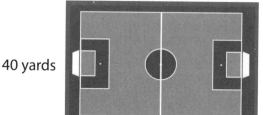

60 yards

40 yards   40 yards

60 yards

a. In problem 1 you found the perimeter of the field. What operation did you use? ....

b. Write an equation you could use to find the perimeter of the field.

c. You can find the perimeter of shapes other than rectangles. Find the perimeter of this shape.

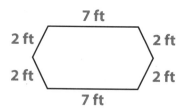

7 ft

2 ft   2 ft

2 ft   2 ft

7 ft

③ REFLECT

Richard wants to put a fence around his backyard. Does he need to find the area or the perimeter of his backyard? What does he need to do to figure out how much fence he needs?

....

....

....

Prepare for Area and Perimeter of Shapes

1. Think about what you know about perimeter. Fill in each box. Use words, numbers, and pictures. Show as many ideas as you can.

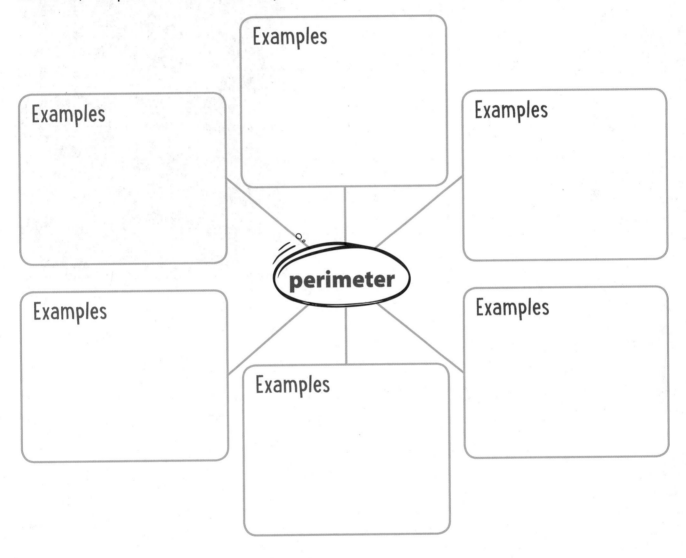

Examples

Examples

Examples

perimeter

Examples

Examples

Examples

2. Write an equation you could use to find the perimeter of the rectangle. What is the perimeter?

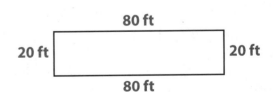

80 ft

20 ft   20 ft

80 ft

3 Solve the problem. Show your work.

Xuan walks the pathway around the field shown. He walks around the whole field one time. How far does Xuan walk?

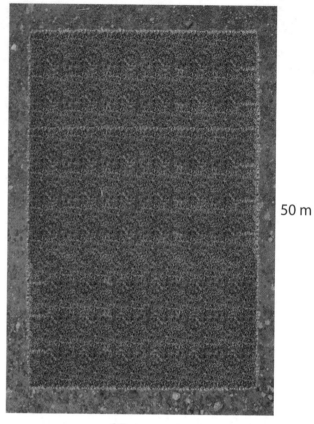

35 m

50 m

50 m

35 m

Solution ....

4 Check your answer. Show your work.

Develop Finding an Unknown Side Length

Read and try to solve the problem below.

> **Willis makes a pen for his rabbit.**
>
> • **The pen has 6 sides.**
>
> • **The perimeter is 10 meters.**
>
> • **The lengths of five of the sides are 1 meter, 3 meters, 2 meters, 1 meter, and 1 meter.**
>
> **What is the length of the sixth side?**

TRY IT

 Math Toolkit
- base-ten blocks
- geoboards
- rubber bands
- grid paper
- number lines
- perimeter and area tool

 **DISCUSS IT**

Ask your partner: How did you get started?

Tell your partner: I started by . . .

Lesson 32 Area and Perimeter of Shapes   **715**

Explore different ways to understand finding an unknown side length.

Willis makes a pen for his rabbit.

• **The pen has 6 sides.**

• **The perimeter is 10 meters.**

• **The lengths of five of the sides are 1 meter, 3 meters, 2 meters, 1 meter, and 1 meter.**

What is the length of the sixth side?

PICTURE IT

You can draw a model to help understand the problem.

The six-sided figure below shows a possible shape of the rabbit pen. The side lengths you know are labeled.

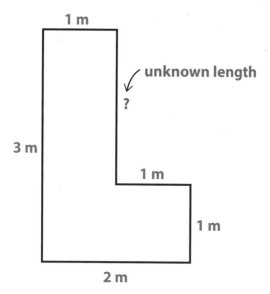

The perimeter of the pen is 10 meters.

CONNECT IT
Now you will use the problem from the previous page to help you understand how to find an unknown side length.

1 Explain how you would find the perimeter of the shape if you knew all of the side lengths.

2 You know the perimeter is 10 meters. Explain how you could figure out the unknown side length.

3 Write an equation to find the unknown side length. Use a ? for the number you do not know.

4 What is the length of the sixth side?

5 Explain how an addition equation can help you find the perimeter of a shape.

6 REFLECT

Look back at your Try It, strategies by classmates, and Picture It. Which models or strategies do you like best for finding an unknown side length? Explain.

....

....

....

....

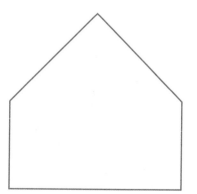

APPLY IT

Use what you just learned to solve these problems.

7 Jordan has a kite with four sides. Two of the sides are 8 inches long. Two of the sides are 12 inches long. What is the perimeter of the kite? Show your work.

Solution ....

8 The perimeter of this shape is 18 feet. What is the unknown side length? Show your work.

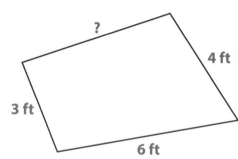

Solution ....

9 Hannah forms 34 inches of wire into the shape of a 5-sided house. Two of the sides are each 5 inches long and two of the sides are each 7 inches long. How long is the last side? Show your work.

Solution ....

Practice Finding an Unknown Side Length

Study the Example showing how to use perimeter to find the unknown side length of a shape. Then solve problems 1–8.

EXAMPLE

This is a floor plan of the shed that Sean is going to build. The perimeter of the shed is 16 meters. What is the unknown side length?

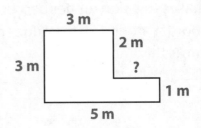

The perimeter is 16 meters. That means that the sum of all the side lengths is 16.

$$5 + 3 + 3 + 2 + 1 + ? = 16$$

$$14 + ? = 16, \text{ so } ? = 2.$$

The unknown side length is 2 meters.

---

1) Write an equation to find the perimeter of this rectangle.

2) The perimeter of this triangle is 12 feet. How can you find the unknown side length? What is the length?

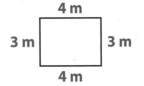

3) A square has a perimeter of 20 inches. Explain how to find the length of each side.

Vocabulary

perimeter the distance around a shape. The perimeter is equal to the sum of the lengths of the sides.

4   Lorenzo knows that the perimeter of this trapezoid is
18 centimeters. Show how to find the length of the top side.
Write the length in the blank.

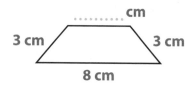

5   Nadia makes this sign for her bedroom door. She wants to put a
ribbon border around all the edges of the sign. She has 12 inches
of ribbon. Is this enough?

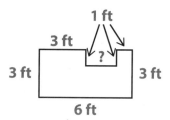

6   The perimeter of this shape is 20 feet. Show how to find the
unknown side length.

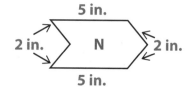

7   Jeff has a garden in the shape of a hexagon. Each of the 6 sides of
the hexagon is 6 feet long. What is the perimeter of the garden?

8   A rectangle has 2 sides that are each 6 centimeters long. The perimeter is
22 centimeters. How long are the other two sides? Show your work.

Solution

Develop Finding Same Area with Different Perimeter

Read and try to solve the problem below.

> **Emma drew the rectangle shown. What other rectangles have the same area, but different perimeters?**

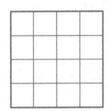

TRY IT

 Math Toolkit
- unit tiles
- geoboards
- rubber bands
- grid paper
- sticky notes
- perimeter and area tool

DISCUSS IT

Ask your partner: How did you get started?

Tell your partner: I knew ... So I ...

Explore different ways to understand finding rectangles with the same area and different perimeters.

> Emma drew the rectangle shown. What other rectangles have the same area, but different perimeters?

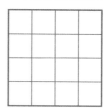

PICTURE IT

You can use drawings to help you find rectangles with the same area and different perimeters.

The area of Emma's rectangle is 16 square units. Below are two other rectangles that also have an area of 16 square units.

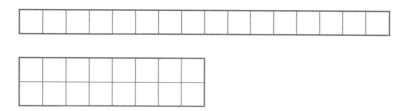

You can also turn these rectangles on their sides to get two more rectangles.

MODEL IT

You can use a table to help you find rectangles with the same area and different perimeters.

You can make a table showing the measurements of rectangles that have an area of 16 square units. The rectangle Emma drew is circled.

Length	Width	Area	Perimeter
16 units	1 unit	16 square units	34 units
8 units	2 units	16 square units	20 units
4 units	4 units	16 square units	16 units
2 units	8 units	16 square units	20 units
1 unit	16 units	16 square units	34 units

CONNECT IT

Now you will use the problem from the previous page to help you understand how to find rectangles with the same area and different perimeters.

1 Look at **Picture It**. How can you tell the two rectangles shown have the same area as Emma's rectangle?

2 To find other rectangles with an area of 16 square units, think of multiplication facts with a product of 16. What are the multiplication facts that have a product of 16?

Look at the table in **Model It**. Where do you see the factors and products of the multiplication facts you wrote?

3 How can two rectangles have the same area but have different perimeters?

4 REFLECT

Look back at your **Try It**, strategies by classmates, and **Picture It** and **Model It**. Which models or strategies do you like best for finding rectangles with the same area and different perimeters? Explain.

....

....

....

....

Lesson 32 Area and Perimeter of Shapes   **723**

APPLY IT

Use what you just learned to solve these problems.

5 Look at the rectangle shown. Draw a rectangle that has the same area but a different perimeter. Show your work.

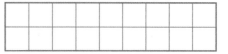

6 Look at the rectangle you drew for problem 5. Is its perimeter the same as, greater than, or less than the perimeter of the original rectangle?

Solution ....

7 Joel plans to start a rectangular garden like the one shown. He wants to put fencing around his garden, but has only 20 feet of fencing. Using the same area as this garden, what side lengths could his garden have so it has a perimeter of 20 feet? Show your work.

3 ft

8 ft

Solution ....

Name: _____

Practice Finding Same Area with Different Perimeter

Study the Example showing how rectangles with the same area can have different perimeters. Then solve problems 1–5.

EXAMPLE

Chang has 12 square tiles. He uses the tiles to make two different rectangles that each have an area of 6 square units. Do these rectangles have the same perimeter?

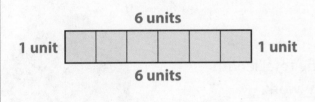

$$6 + 1 + 6 + 1 = 14$$
perimeter = 14 units

$$3 + 2 + 3 + 2 = 10$$
perimeter = 10 units

Rectangles with the same area can have different perimeters.

1 Both rectangles on the right have an area of 12 square units. Write the perimeter of each in the table.

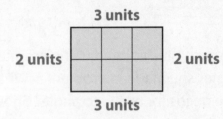

Length	Width	Area	Perimeter
6 units	2 units	12 square units	units
4 units	3 units	12 square units	units

2 Draw two different rectangles that have an area of 10 square units. Write the number of units for each length, width, and perimeter.

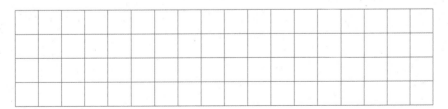

1: length = ..., width = ..., perimeter = ...

2: length = ..., width = ..., perimeter = ...

3   Simone has 16 square-inch tiles. She glues all of them on cardboard to make two different rectangles, each with the same area. What are the side lengths of two rectangles she can make? Show your work.

Solution ....

4   Simone wants to glue colored string around the edges of the two rectangles she made in problem 3. What is the total length of string she needs for each rectangle? Show your work.

Solution ....

5   Enrique draws the rectangle at the right. Draw another rectangle with the same area but a different perimeter. Which rectangle has the greater perimeter?

©Curriculum Associates, LLC   Copying is not permitted.

Develop Finding Same Perimeter with Different Area

Read and try to solve the problem below.

> **Kai drew the rectangle shown. What other rectangles have the same perimeter, but different areas?**

TRY IT

 Math Toolkit
- unit tiles
- geoboards
- rubber bands
- grid paper
- number lines
- perimeter and area tool

DISCUSS IT

Ask your partner: Why did you choose that strategy?

Tell your partner: The strategy I used to find the answer was . . .

Explore different ways to understand finding rectangles with the same perimeter and different areas.

> **Kai drew the rectangle shown. What other rectangles have the same perimeter, but different areas?**

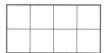

PICTURE IT

You can use drawings to help you find rectangles with the same perimeter and different areas.

The perimeter of Kai's rectangle is 12 units. All of the rectangles below have a perimeter of 12 units.

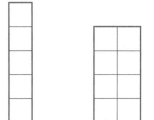

MODEL IT

You can use a table to help you find rectangles with the same perimeter and different areas.

The table below shows the measurements of rectangles that have a perimeter of 12 units. The rectangle Kai drew is circled.

Length	Width	Area	Perimeter
3 units	3 units	9 square units	12 units
4 units	2 units	8 square units	12 units
5 units	1 unit	5 square units	12 units

CONNECT IT

Now you will use the problem from the previous page to help you understand how to find rectangles with the same perimeter and different areas.

1 Look at the table in Model It. What do you notice about the sum of the length and the width of each rectangle?

How does the sum of the length and width compare to the perimeter?

2 All of the rectangles have the same perimeter as Kai's rectangle. Explain why only one has the same area as Kai's rectangle.

3 List the measurements of the rectangles that have the same perimeter but different areas than Kai's rectangle.

4 How can two rectangles have the same perimeter but have different areas?

5 REFLECT

Look back at your Try It, strategies by classmates, and Picture It and Model It. Which models or strategies do you like best for finding rectangles with the same perimeter and different areas? Explain.

....

....

....

APPLY IT

Use what you just learned to solve these problems.

6 Look at the rectangle shown. Draw a rectangle that has the same perimeter but a different area. Show your work.

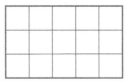

7 Look at the rectangle you drew for problem 6. Is its area the same as, greater than, or less than the area of the original rectangle?

Solution ....

8 Marc is weaving a new rectangular rug that has the same perimeter and different area of an old rug. The old rug is 9 feet long and 4 feet wide. If the new rug is 6 feet wide, how long is it? What is the area of the new rug? Show your work.

4 feet

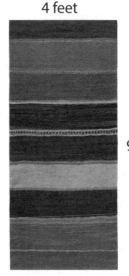

9 feet

Solution ....

Practice Finding Same Perimeter with Different Area

Study the Example showing that rectangles with the same perimeter can have different areas. Then solve problems 1–6.

EXAMPLE

Kat draws two different rectangles, each with a perimeter of 10 units. Do these rectangles have the same area?

length = 4 units and width = 1 unit   length = 3 units and width = 2 units
    area = 4 square units   area = 6 square units

Rectangles with the same perimeter can have different areas.

---

1 Both rectangular banners on the right have a perimeter of 14 feet. Write the area of each in the table.

Length	Width	Area	Perimeter
6 feet	1 foot		14 feet
5 feet	2 feet		14 feet

2 Draw a different rectangle that has a perimeter of 14 feet. Write the length, width, and area in the table.

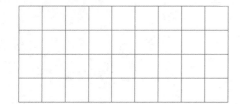

Each ☐ = 1 square foot.

Length	Width	Area	Perimeter
feet	feet	square feet	14 feet

Use Rectangles _A_, _B_, and _C_ for problems 3–5.

3 Which rectangle has the greatest area? Show your work.

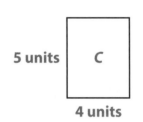

3 units | A | 6 units

Solution ....

4 Which rectangles have the same perimeter? Show your work.

5 units | B | 5 units

Solution ....

5 Draw a rectangle that has the same perimeter as Rectangle _A_ and a different area than Rectangles _A_, _B_, or _C_. Write the length, width, and area of your rectangle.

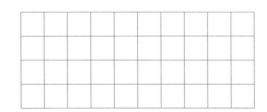

length ....

width ....

area ....

5 units | C | 4 units

6 Find the side lengths of two different rectangles that have a perimeter of 20 units. Then find and compare their areas.

Refine Working with Area and Perimeter of Shapes

Complete the Example below. Then solve problems 1–8.

EXAMPLE

Look at the rectangle below. Draw a rectangle that has the same perimeter but a different area.

6 units

4 units   4 units

6 units

Look at how you could show your work using a drawing.

Rectangle above: length = 6 units and width = 4 units

Try a length of 7 units.

7 + 7 = 14

20 − 14 = 6

6 ÷ 2 = 3

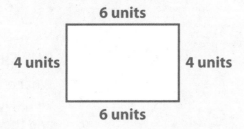

7 units

..... units   ..... units

7 units

The perimeter of the rectangle is 20 units, and the area is 24 square units. The rectangle the student draws needs to have a perimeter of 20 units, too.

PAIR/SHARE
What other rectangles could you draw?

APPLY IT

1 Jared's dad builds a square deck in his backyard. One side of the deck is 10 feet long. What is the perimeter of the deck? Show your work.

The sides of a square are all the same length. How many sides do you need to add together to find the perimeter?

PAIR/SHARE
What equation could you write to find the perimeter?

Solution ....

2 Belinda's rectangular side yard is shown below. Draw a rectangle that has the same area as the yard but a different perimeter. Show your work.

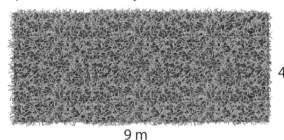

4 m

9 m

The area is 4 meters × 9 meters, or 36 square meters. What numbers, other than 4 and 9, are factors of 36?

PAIR/SHARE
What other rectangle would have the same area and the same perimeter?

3 The perimeter of the shape below is 12 centimeters.

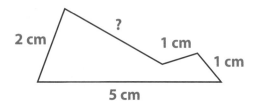

2 cm

?

1 cm

1 cm

5 cm

You could write an equation with a ? for the unknown number to show the perimeter.

What is the unknown side length?

Ⓐ 2 cm

Ⓑ 3 cm

Ⓒ 4 cm

Ⓓ 9 cm

Rose chose Ⓓ as the correct answer. How did she get that answer?

PAIR/SHARE
Does Rose's answer make sense?

4 Rachel has 20 feet of fencing to put around a rectangular section of her lawn. The fencing must go around the perimeter of the rectangular section with no overlap. Does Rachel have exactly enough fencing for each rectangular section shown below? The area of each ☐ is 1 square foot.

	Yes	No
	Ⓐ	Ⓑ
	Ⓒ	Ⓓ
	Ⓔ	Ⓕ
	Ⓖ	Ⓗ

5 Ling plants a flower garden and a vegetable garden. Both gardens are rectangles.

Part A Ling's flower garden is 8 feet long. It has an area of 40 square feet. What is the perimeter of the flower garden? Show your work.

Part B Ling's vegetable garden is 10 feet wide. Its area is the same as the flower garden. Which garden has the greater perimeter? Show your work.

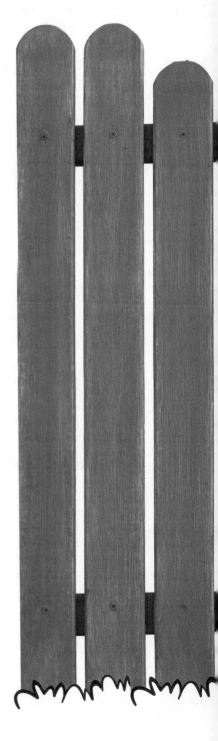

6 Look at Rectangle *A* below. The area of each ☐ is 1 square unit.

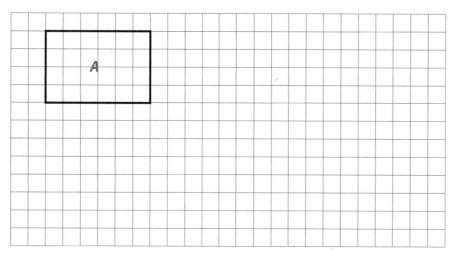

Part A Find the perimeter and area of Rectangle *A*.

Perimeter: .... units   Area: .... square units

Part B Use the grid to draw a rectangle that has the same perimeter but a different area than Rectangle *A*. Label it Rectangle *B*. Write the perimeter and area of Rectangle *B*.

Perimeter: .... units   Area: .... square units

Part C Use the grid to draw a rectangle that has the same area but a different perimeter than Rectangle *A*. Label it Rectangle *C*. Write the perimeter and area of Rectangle *C*.

Perimeter: .... units   Area: .... square units

7 MATH JOURNAL

Alex says that all rectangles with a perimeter of 14 meters have the same area. Is she correct? Explain.

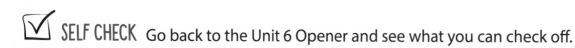

SELF CHECK Go back to the Unit 6 Opener and see what you can check off.

Partition Shapes into Parts with Equal Areas

Dear Family,

This week your child is learning about breaking shapes into parts that have equal areas.

Equal parts of a shape cover an equal area. Think of these parts as fractions of the whole area.

These squares are broken into 4 equal parts each. So, the area of one shaded part is $\frac{1}{4}$ of the area of the whole square.

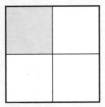 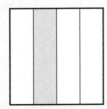 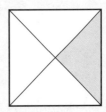

Since all 4 parts in each square are the same size and shape, each part is $\frac{1}{4}$ of the whole shape.

Here the square is broken into 8 equal parts.

So, the area of one part is $\frac{1}{8}$ of the whole.

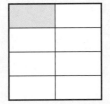

Invite your child to share what he or she knows about dividing shapes into parts with equal areas by doing the following activity together.

ACTIVITY DIVIDING SHAPES INTO EQUAL AREAS

Do this activity with your child to practice dividing shapes into equal parts.

Materials 2 sheets of paper, crayons or markers

Do this activity with your child to give him or her practice dividing a rectangle into equal parts.

- Work with your child to fold a sheet of paper to make parts with equal areas. Begin by helping your child fold a piece of paper in thirds.

- Guide your child to fold the piece of paper one more time in half, then open the sheet of paper.

- Ask your child the following questions.

  1. How many equal parts do you see?

  2. What is a fraction that names one section?

  Then have him or her color $\frac{2}{6}$ of the rectangle.

- Now, together fold another sheet of paper in the exact same way and color $\frac{2}{6}$ in a different way.

- Challenge:

  3. What is an equivalent fraction for $\frac{2}{6}$, based on the part of the whole that is colored?

Answers: **1.** 6 equal parts; **2.** $\frac{1}{6}$; **3.** $\frac{1}{3}$

Explore Partitioning Shapes into Parts with Equal Areas

You have learned about equivalent fractions, equal parts of shapes, and finding area. In this lesson you will learn how to break apart shapes into parts with equal area. Use what you know to try to solve the problem below.

Learning Target
- Partition shapes into parts with equal areas. Express the area of each part as a unit fraction of the whole.

SMP 1, 2, 3, 4, 5, 6, 7

Use different ways to break each square into two equal parts. Shade one part of each square. What unit fraction could you use to describe the shaded part? Explain how you know.

TRY IT

 **Math Toolkit**
- unit tiles
- grid paper
- dot paper
- sticky notes
- fraction models

DISCUSS IT

Ask your partner: Why did you choose that strategy?

Tell your partner: The strategy I used to find the answer was . . .

CONNECT IT

1 LOOK BACK

Explain how you know the unit fraction that names the shaded part of each square.

2 LOOK AHEAD

You can break apart the same shape into equal parts in a lot of ways. You can use fractions to describe the area that each part covers. Look at the rectangles below. The shaded areas of all four rectangles are both alike and different.

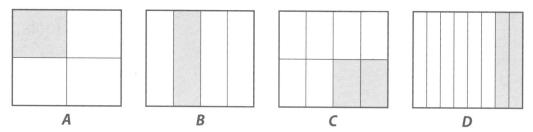

A   B   C   D

a. What fraction of the area of rectangle *A* is shaded? ....

What fraction of the area of rectangle *B* is shaded? ....

What fraction of the area of rectangle *C* is shaded? ....

What fraction of the area of rectangle *D* is shaded? ....

b. For rectangles *C* and *D*, what unit fraction is equivalent to the fraction shown

by the shaded parts? ....

3 REFLECT

What is the same about the areas shown by the shading in the four rectangles above? What is different?

....

....

....

Prepare for Partitioning Shapes into Parts with Equal Areas

1 Think about what you know about fractions and shapes. Fill in each box.
Use words, numbers, and pictures. Show as many ideas as you can.

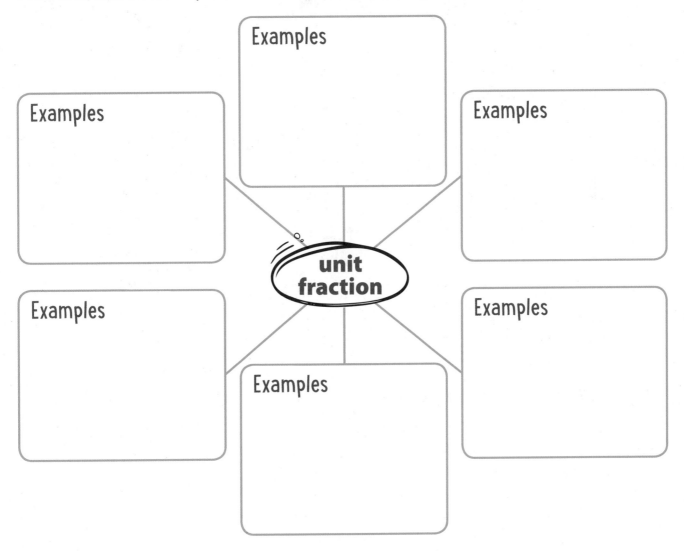

Examples

Examples

Examples

Examples

Examples

Examples

unit fraction

2 Look at the rectangle below.

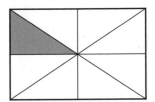

What unit fraction names the shaded part of the rectangle? ....

3) Solve the problem. Show your work.

Use different ways to break each square below into four equal parts. Shade one part of each square. What unit fraction could you use to describe the shaded part? Explain how you know.

☐ ☐ ☐

Solution ....

....

4) Check your answer. Show your work.

Develop Partitioning Shapes into Equal Parts

Read and try to solve the problem below.

Brett folded a piece of paper three times as shown. He then colored $\frac{1}{4}$ of the total area of the paper red. How could he have colored his paper?

Explain how you know your way is right.

TRY IT

🧰 **Math Toolkit**
- fraction tiles
- grid paper
- colored pencils
- fraction models 🖱

DISCUSS IT

Ask your partner: Do you agree with me? Why or why not?

Tell your partner: I agree with you about . . . because . . .

Explore different ways to understand dividing shapes into equal parts.

> **Brett folded a piece of paper three times as shown. He then colored $\frac{1}{4}$ of the total area of the paper red. How could he have colored his paper?**
>
> **Explain how you know your way is right.**

MODEL IT

You can act out the problem and make a model.

Fold a piece of paper in half three times as Brett did.

Unfold the paper.

This is what the paper looks like, divided into equal parts.

SOLVE IT

You can use equivalent fractions to solve the problem.

The paper has 8 equal parts.

You need to color a number of parts red so that $\frac{1}{4}$ of the area of the paper is colored.

Think of a fraction equivalent to $\frac{1}{4}$ to help solve the problem. You can compare numbers using $<$, $>$, or $=$. Since your fraction will be equivalent to $\frac{1}{4}$, you can compare the fractions using $=$.

CONNECT IT

Now you will use the problem from the previous page to help you understand how to divide shapes into equal parts.

1 How many equal parts are on the paper? .... How many in 1 row? ....

Suppose Brett colors 1 row. What fraction of the paper does he color? ....

What fraction of the paper is NOT colored? ....

Use $<$, $>$, or $=$ to compare the fraction of the paper that is colored and the fraction that is not colored. $\frac{2}{8}$ ◯ $\frac{6}{8}$

2 What fraction of the paper is 1 row? Explain.

3 Does Brett color $\frac{1}{4}$ of the area of the paper? Use your answers above to explain.

4 How else could Brett have colored $\frac{1}{4}$ of the paper?

5 To color $\frac{1}{4}$ of the paper, must Brett color parts that are next to each other? Explain.

6 REFLECT

Look back at your **Try It**, strategies by classmates, and **Model It** and **Solve It**. Which models or strategies do you like best for dividing shapes into equal parts? Explain.

....

....

....

APPLY IT

Use what you just learned to solve these problems.

7 Divide this rectangle into 8 equal parts. What fraction of the total area of the rectangle is each part?

Solution ....

8 Show a different way to divide the rectangle from problem 7 into 8 equal parts. What fraction of the total area of the rectangle is each part?

Solution ....

9 Each shape is divided into equal parts. Which shapes show $\frac{1}{2}$ of the area shaded?

Ⓐ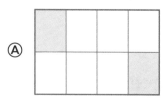

Ⓑ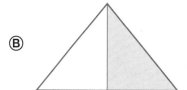

Ⓒ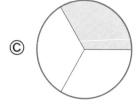

Ⓓ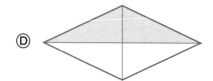

Ⓔ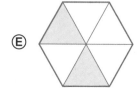

Ⓕ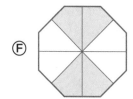

Practice Partitioning Shapes into Equal Parts

Study the Example showing how to divide rectangles into equal parts. Then solve problems 1–10.

EXAMPLE

Brad and Linda each cover a same-sized board with mosaic tiles. Here are the designs they made. What part of Brad's design is red tiles? What part of Linda's design is red tiles?

Brad's Design

Linda's Design

2 rows of 4 tiles = 8 tiles

$\frac{4}{8}$, or $\frac{1}{2}$, of the tiles are red.

4 rows of 2 tiles = 8 tiles

$\frac{4}{8}$, or $\frac{1}{2}$, of the tiles are red.

1 How many equal parts are in rectangle *A*? ....

2 How many rows are in rectangle *A*? ....

3 What fraction of the total area of rectangle *A* is shaded? ....

4 Use rectangle *B* to show another way to divide a rectangle into

6 equal parts. What unit fraction is each part? ....

5 What fraction of the total area of rectangle *C* is shaded?
Tell how you know.

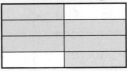

A

B

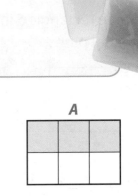

C

6 The octagon is divided into equal parts. What fraction of the total
area of the octagon is each part? ·················

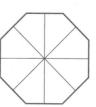

7 Compare squares *X* and *Y*. Tell whether each statement is *True* or *False*.

X

	True	False
$\frac{1}{2}$ of shape *X* is shaded.	Ⓐ	Ⓑ
$\frac{1}{2}$ of shape *Y* is shaded.	Ⓒ	Ⓓ
Each row of shape *X* is $\frac{1}{4}$ of the whole square.	Ⓔ	Ⓕ
Each row of shape *Y* is $\frac{1}{4}$ the whole square.	Ⓖ	Ⓗ

Y

8 Divide rectangle *S* into 4 equal parts and divide rectangle *T* into
8 equal parts.

S

T

9 Shade $\frac{1}{4}$ of the area of each rectangle in problem 8.

10 Use <, >, or = to compare the shaded parts of the rectangles in problem 8.

$\frac{1}{4}$ ◯ ·········

11 Divide the hexagon into 6 equal triangles. Then shade $\frac{1}{2}$ or $\frac{1}{3}$ of the
area of the hexagon. Tell how you know $\frac{1}{2}$ or $\frac{1}{3}$ of the area is shaded.

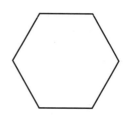

Complete the Example below. Then solve problems 1–8.

EXAMPLE

A rectangular game board is divided into same-sized squares. There are 4 rows. Each row has 2 squares. What fraction of the total area of the game board does each row cover?

Look at how you could show your work using a model.

1 row out of 4 rows is shaded.

Solution ....

> The student used a grid to make a model of the game board.

PAIR/SHARE
How could you solve the problem without using a model?

APPLY IT

1 The triangle is divided into equal parts. How does the area of one part compare to the area of the whole triangle? Shade $\frac{1}{2}$ of the triangle.

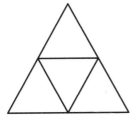

Solution ....

> How many smaller triangles are there?

PAIR/SHARE
What is a different way to shade $\frac{1}{2}$ of the triangle?

2 Shade $\frac{1}{3}$ of the circle below. How many same-sized parts cover $\frac{1}{3}$ of the circle? Show your work.

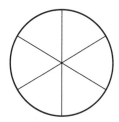

Remember that $\frac{1}{3}$ means 1 out of 3 equal parts.

Solution ....

PAIR/SHARE
What fraction of the whole circle is each part?

3 A rectangle is equally divided into 2 rows. Each row is divided into 3 same-sized squares. What fraction of the total area of the rectangle is each square?

Ⓐ $\frac{1}{2}$

Ⓑ $\frac{1}{3}$

Ⓒ $\frac{1}{4}$

Ⓓ $\frac{1}{6}$

Ben chose Ⓐ as the correct answer. How did he get that answer?

How many squares are in the whole rectangle?

PAIR/SHARE
What do you think Ben was thinking when he chose his answer?

4 A rectangle is divided into same-sized squares. Four of the squares are shaded. The area of the shaded parts is $\frac{1}{2}$ the area of the whole rectangle. How many squares make up the whole rectangle?

Ⓐ 2 squares

Ⓑ 4 squares

Ⓒ 8 squares

Ⓓ 16 squares

5 A rectangle is divided into 6 same-sized squares. How many squares cover $\frac{1}{2}$ of the area of the rectangle?

6 The rectangles below are all the same size. Dani wants to shade $\frac{1}{3}$ of the area of each rectangle. Use the rectangles below to show three different ways to shade $\frac{1}{3}$.

  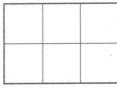

How many squares do you need to shade to cover $\frac{1}{3}$ of the area of one of the rectangles?

.... squares

7 Divide each octagon into 4 equal parts. Then shade one or more parts of each to show two different unit fractions. Write the fraction under each octagon. Then compare the fractions using <, >, or =.

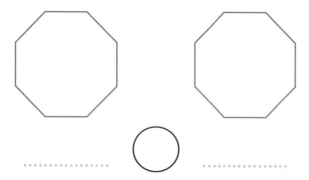

8 MATH JOURNAL

Suppose you divide a hexagon into 6 equal parts. Explain how you could shade the parts to show three different unit fractions.

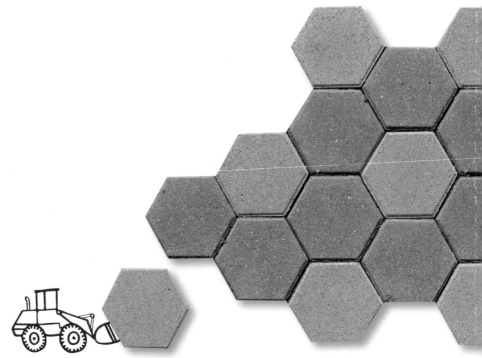

☑ SELF CHECK Go back to the Unit 6 Opener and see what you can check off.

In this unit you learned to . . .

Skill	Lesson
Describe shapes, compare them, and put them in groups that tell how they are alike, for example: by the number of sides or by whether they have right angles.	30, 31
Compare quadrilaterals and put them in groups based on their attributes, for example: all 4 sides are the same length or there are 2 pairs of parallel sides.	31
Solve problems involving perimeters, including finding an unknown side length, and finding rectangles with the same perimeter and different areas or with the same area and different perimeters.	32
Divide rectangles into parts with equal area and name the area of shaded parts using unit fractions.	33

Think about what you learned.

Use words, numbers, and drawings.

1 Two things I learned in math are . . .

2 Something I know well is . . .

3 I could use more practice with . . .

Work with Shapes

Study an Example Problem and Solution

SMP 1 Make sense of problems and persevere in solving them.

Read this problem about shapes. Then look at Bella's solution to this problem.

Paper Shapes

Bella recycles colored paper and wrapping paper. She cuts the paper into different shapes. She saves the shapes for crafts. Sometimes she looks for pieces with certain kinds of sides. Sometimes she looks for shapes with certain kinds of angles. Bella needs to sort the shapes shown below.

Show a way to sort all of the shapes. You can group shapes by their sides or by their angles. Make at least two groups. Be sure every shape belongs to at least one group. Put each shape into every group it fits in.

Read the sample solution on the next page. Then look at the checklist below. Find and mark parts of the solution that match the checklist.

☑ PROBLEM-SOLVING CHECKLIST

- ☐ Tell what is known.
- ☐ Tell what the problem is asking.
- ☐ Show all your work.
- ☐ Show that the solution works.

a. Circle something that is known.

b. Underline something that you need to find.

c. Draw a box around what you do to solve the problem.

d. Put a checkmark next to the part that shows the solution works.

BELLA'S SOLUTION

Hi, I'm Bella. Here's how I solved the problem.

- **I see some shapes with . . .**

  - 3 sides, 4 sides, 5 sides, and 6 sides.

  - sides that are the same length.

  - sides that are all different.

- **I also see shapes with . . .**

  - 3 angles, 4 angles, 5 angles, and 6 angles.

  - square corners.

  - no square corners.

First I looked at what kinds of shapes there are.

- **I will sort the shapes into two groups.**

  I will make one group of shapes that have some sides the same length.

  I will make one group of shapes with no square corners.

A table is a good way to show groups.

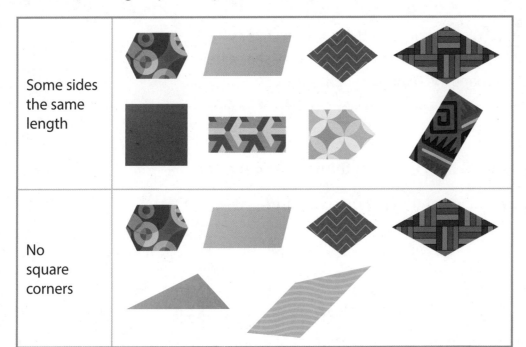

8 shapes are in one group.
6 shapes are in the other group.
4 shapes are in both groups.
All of the shapes are used at least once.

Try Another Approach

Some problems have more than one answer. Think about how to find a different answer for the Paper Shapes problem.

Paper Shapes

Bella recycles colored paper and wrapping paper. She cuts the paper into different shapes. She saves the shapes for crafts. Sometimes she looks for pieces with certain kinds of sides. Sometimes she looks for shapes with certain kinds of angles. Bella needs to sort the shapes shown below.

Show a way to sort all of the shapes. You can group shapes by their sides or by their angles. Make at least two groups. Be sure every shape belongs to at least one group. Put each shape into every group it fits in.

PLAN IT

Answer these questions to help you start thinking about a plan.

A. What are some of the different groups you could use?

B. How could one shape be in two different groups?

SOLVE IT

Find a different solution for the Paper Shapes problem. Show all your work on a separate sheet of paper.

You may want to use the Problem-Solving Tips to get started.

PROBLEM-SOLVING TIPS

- **Tools** You may want to use . . .

  - a table.

  - grid paper.

- **Word Bank**

sides	square corner	length
angles	opposite sides	

- **Sentence Starters**

- _____ has sides that are _____

- The angles in _____

✓ PROBLEM-SOLVING CHECKLIST

Make sure that you . . .
- ☐ tell what you know.
- ☐ tell what you need to do.
- ☐ show all your work.
- ☐ show that the solution works.

REFLECT

Use Mathematical Practices Choose one of these questions to discuss with a partner.

- **Use Tools** What tools could help you tell about the sides and angles of the shapes?

- **Be Precise** What are some of the different words you can use to name the shapes in this problem?

Discuss Models and Strategies

Read the problem. Write a solution on a separate sheet of paper. Remember, there can be lots of ways to solve a problem!

Cut Squares

Bella has some square pieces of paper that are all the same size. She plans to cut each square into equal parts. Then she will sort the parts by shape.

Here are Bella's notes about how she wants to cut the squares.

My Notes

- Cut each square into the same number of equal parts.
- Make 4 or more equal parts from each square.
- Each square should be cut into equal parts that look different than the equal parts from the other squares.

How should Bella cut her squares?

PLAN IT AND SOLVE IT

Find a solution for the Cut Squares problem.

Help Bella decide how to cut the squares.

• Pick a number of equal parts.

• Divide the four squares into that number of equal parts in different ways.

• Write the fraction that can be used to name one equal part.

• List all of the shape names that can be used to describe the equal parts for each square.

You may want to use the Problem-Solving Tips to get started.

PROBLEM-SOLVING TIPS

● **Questions**

  • How can you describe the sides of the smaller shapes you made?

  • What do the angles in your shapes look like?

● **Word Bank**

quadrilateral	rectangle	measure
triangle	square	fraction

☑ **PROBLEM-SOLVING CHECKLIST**

Make sure that you . . .

☐ tell what you know.

☐ tell what you need to do.

☐ show all your work.

☐ show that the solution works.

REFLECT

Use Mathematical Practices Choose one of these questions to discuss with a partner.

• **Use Tools** What tools can you use to draw the equal parts? How can you use these tools?

• **Critique Reasoning** Tell your partner how you named your shapes. Do you agree with each other? Tell why or why not.

Persevere On Your Own

Read the problems. Write a solution on a separate sheet of paper.

Rectangular Snack Trays

At the community center Bella meets an artist who weaves trays. Bella asks the artist to make two snack trays for her. Bella's ideas are shown below.

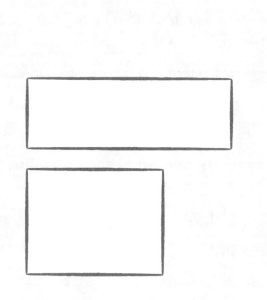

My Ideas

- Each tray is shaped like a rectangle.
- Both trays have the same area.
- The perimeter of each tray is different.
- The area of each tray is less than 100 square inches.

What size trays can Bella ask the artist to make?

SOLVE IT

Help Bella decide what size trays to ask for.

- Choose an area that is less than 100 square inches.
- Show two different ways to make this area.
- Find the perimeter of each rectangle and show that they are different.

REFLECT

Use Mathematical Practices Choose one of these questions to discuss with a partner.

- **Persevere** How did you choose the number you used for the area?
- **Be Precise** How did you check that your solution was correct?

Bella's Show

Bella is planning a show about mosaic art. She uses small square pieces of paper to make colorful designs. At the show, people can enter a mosaic design contest. Here are the rules for the contest.

Design 1

- Use up to 48 squares.
- Put the squares in equal rows.

Design 2

- Use the same number of squares as Design 1.
- Make a rectangle with a different perimeter.

What are two designs you could enter in the contest?

SOLVE IT

Enter Bella's mosaic contest.

Follow Bella's rules to make two different drawings.

- Choose a number of squares to use.

- Make two drawings.

- Write multiplication equations to show the number of rows, the number of squares in each row, and the total number of squares.

- Write equations to show the perimeter of each design.

REFLECT

Use Mathematical Practices Choose one of these questions to discuss with a partner.

- **Reason Mathematically** How did you choose the number of squares to use?

- **Use a Model** How does each equation you wrote relate to the design?

1 Rami sorts shapes into groups. Which shape belongs in the group *4 right angles*?

Ⓐ

Ⓑ

Ⓒ

Ⓓ

2 Which words can be used to describe the shape at the right? Choose all the correct answers.

Ⓐ right triangle

Ⓑ parallelogram

Ⓒ rectangle

Ⓓ rhombus

Ⓔ square

3 Abbie places a desk and table together to form the shape below. The perimeter is 36 meters. What is the unknown side length in meters? Show your work.

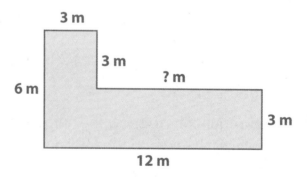

3 m

3 m

? m

6 m

3 m

12 m

4 Dae knits a scarf in the shape of a rectangle. The scarf is 8 inches wide. Its area is 480 square inches. What is the perimeter of his scarf? Show your work.

Solution ....

5 Complete the table by writing the letters of the shapes that belong in each group. Some shapes may belong to more than one group.

At Least 1 Right Angle	Is a Parallelogram	All Sides the Same Length

6 Adrick divides a rectangle into 2 equal rows with 4 squares in each row. What fraction of Adrick's rectangle is covered by 2 squares? Show your work.

Solution ....

Performance Task

Answer the questions and show all your work on separate paper.

Read each riddle below. Use the clues to draw the shape or shapes you think they describe. Name the shapes when possible. A riddle may have more than one answer.

1. I am a four-sided shape. What could I be?

2. I am a four-sided shape. I have two pairs of parallel sides. What could I be?

3. I am a four-sided shape. I have two pairs of parallel sides. All of my sides are the same length. What could I be?

4. I am a four-sided shape. I have two pairs of parallel sides. All of my sides are the same length. I have four right angles. What could I be?

> ### Checklist
> Did you . . .
> ☐ write at least 3 clues for each chosen shape?
> ☐ use vocabulary from the unit?
> ☐ draw all the shapes possible for each riddle?

Choose two of the shapes below. Write a riddle for each shape. Use vocabulary from the unit. Each riddle should have at least three clues.

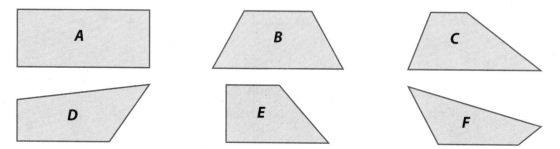

Choose a partner and read the clues for one of your shapes out loud. Have your partner draw the shape they think the clues describe. Does your partner's drawing match the shape you chose? Explain how the shape you chose and the shape your partner drew can be different, even if your partner did not make a mistake.

REFLECT

Use Mathematical Practices After you complete the task, choose one of the following questions to answer.

• **Be Precise** List all of the geometry words you used to write your clues. What does each word mean?

• **Use Tools** What tools could you use to make accurate drawings of your shapes? Why would you need each of these tools?

Draw or write to show examples for each term. Then draw or write to show other math words in the unit.

attribute any characteristic of an object or shape, such as number of sides or angles, lengths of sides, or angle measures.

My Example

parallel always the same distance apart.

My Example

parallelogram a quadrilateral with opposite sides parallel and equal in length.

My Example

perimeter the distance around a two-dimensional shape. The perimeter is equal to the sum of the lengths of the sides.

My Example

rectangle a quadrilateral with 4 right angles. Opposite sides of a rectangle are the same length.

My Example

right angle an angle that looks like the corner of a square.

My Example

My Word: _____

_____

_____

My Example

My Word: _____

_____

_____

My Example

My Word: _____

_____

_____

My Example

My Word: _____

_____

_____

My Example

My Word: _____

_____

_____

My Example

My Word: _____

_____

_____

My Example

Cumulative Practice

Name: _____

Set 1: Count to Find Area

Count to find the area.

1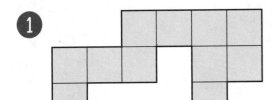

Area = _____ square units

2

Area = _____ square units

3

1 square inch

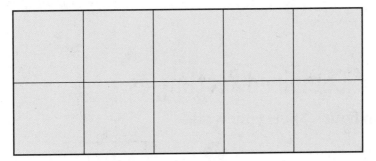

Area = _____ square inches

Set 2: Multiply to Find Area

Solve the problems. Draw to show your work.

1 A rectangle with length 3 inches and width 6 inches. What is the area of the rectangle?

2 A square has sides that are 5 centimeters long. What is the area?

Area = _____ square inches

Area = _____ square centimeters

Set 3: Solve Word Problems About Area

Solve the problems. Show your work.

1 A ping pong table is 9 feet long and 5 feet wide. What is the area of the ping pong table?

2 The top of Jessica's nightstand is 12 inches long and 10 inches wide. The book that is on her nightstand is 8 inches long and 6 inches wide. How much of the top of Jessica's nightstand is NOT covered by the book?

Set 4: Find Areas of Combined Rectangles

Find the total area of each figure. Show your work.

1

6 in.   6 in.

4 in.

Area = _____ square inches

2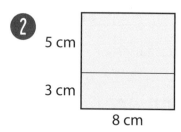

5 cm

3 cm

8 cm

Area = _____ square centimeters

3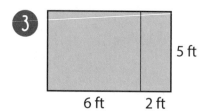

5 ft

6 ft   2 ft

Area = _____ square feet

4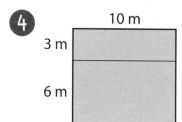

10 m

3 m

6 m

Area = _____ square meters

Set 5: Find Areas of Non-Rectangular Shapes

Find the area of each shape. Show your work.

1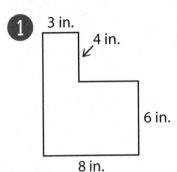

2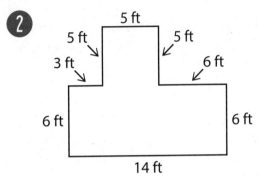

Area = _____ square inches

Area = _____ square feet

Set 6: Solve Word Problems Using Multiplication and Division

Solve the problems. Show your work.

1 The computer lab has 4 rows of computers. There are 7 computers in each row. How many computers are in the computer lab?

_____ computers

2 Quincy has 24 pages of a textbook to read. He has 3 days to finish the reading. If he reads the same number of pages each day, how many pages will he read in one day?

_____ pages

Set 7: Solve Two-Step Word Problems

Solve the problems. Show your work.

1 The drama club raises $230 to put on their next production. They buy 8 yards of fabric at $10 per yard. How much money, *m*, do they have left?

2 Mike has 18 grocery store gift cards. Each gift card has a value of $5. He splits the gift cards evenly among 6 friends. How much money, *g*, does each friend have to spend at the grocery store?

Set 8: Patterns in Numbers

Fill in the blanks with *even* or *odd*.

1 The sum of two even numbers is always _____.

2 The sum of two odd numbers is always _____.

3 The sum of an odd number and an even number is always _____.

Set 9: Multiplication and Division Facts

Solve the problems.

1 $4 \times$ _____ $= 12$

2 $15 \div$ _____ $= 3$

3 _____ $\times 5 = 30$

4 _____ $\div 5 = 5$

5 $3 \times$ _____ $= 18$

6 $24 \div$ _____ $= 8$

7 $3 \times$ _____ $= 27$ $27 \div 9 =$ _____

8 _____ $\times 7 = 42$ $42 \div 6 =$ _____

_____ $\times 3 = 27$ _____ $\div 3 = 9$

$7 \times$ _____ $= 42$ $42 \div$ _____ $= 6$

Cumulative Practice

Name: _____

Set 1: Fractions

Write the fraction of each figure that is shaded for problems 1–3.

 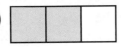 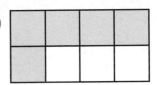

....

Write each fraction in words for problems 4–7.

4 $\frac{1}{2}$ ....

5 $\frac{1}{6}$ ....

6 $\frac{6}{8}$ ....

7 $\frac{3}{6}$ ....

Set 2: Fractions on a Number Line

Identify the fractions that the letters name on each number line.

1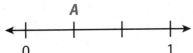

A is ....

2

A is ....

B is ....

3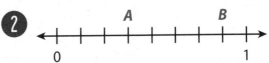

A is ....   *B* is ....   *C* is ....

Set 3: Equivalent Fractions

Use the models to identify equivalent fractions.

1 Label each part of the models. Shade the models to show a fraction equivalent to $\frac{3}{4}$.

$\frac{3}{4} =$ ....

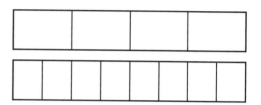

2 Label the number lines. Identify the equivalent fraction.

$\frac{2}{4} =$ ....

Set 4: Find Equivalent Fractions

Fill in the blank to complete the equivalent fraction.

1 $\frac{1}{3} = \frac{\square}{6}$

2 $\frac{1}{2} = \frac{\square}{8}$

3 $\frac{10}{6} = \frac{\square}{3}$

4 $\frac{1}{4} = \frac{\square}{8}$

5 $\frac{4}{6} = \frac{\square}{3}$

6 $\frac{2}{4} = \frac{\square}{2}$

Set 5: Write Whole Numbers as Fractions

Fill in the blank to write a fraction for each whole number in problems 1–6.

1 $1 = \frac{\square}{4}$

2 $1 = \frac{\square}{8}$

3 $1 = \frac{\square}{6}$

4 $4 = \frac{\square}{1}$

5 $2 = \frac{\square}{1}$

6 $2 = \frac{\square}{2}$

Write the whole number for each fraction in problems 7–9.

7 $\frac{7}{1} =$ ....

8 $\frac{1}{1} =$ ....

9 $\frac{3}{1} =$ ....

Set 6: Compare Fractions

Write <, >, or = in each circle to compare the fractions.

1 $\frac{1}{2}$ ◯ $\frac{1}{6}$

2 $\frac{5}{6}$ ◯ $\frac{4}{6}$

3 $\frac{2}{8}$ ◯ $\frac{3}{8}$

4 $\frac{9}{3}$ ◯ $\frac{10}{3}$

5 $\frac{5}{6}$ ◯ $\frac{5}{8}$

6 $\frac{2}{8}$ ◯ $\frac{2}{4}$

7 $\frac{2}{3}$ ◯ $\frac{2}{3}$

8 $\frac{3}{6}$ ◯ $\frac{3}{4}$

9 $\frac{1}{8}$ ◯ $\frac{1}{6}$

Set 7: Multiply to Find Area

Find the area of each shape. Show your work.

1 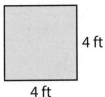 4 ft, 4 ft

2 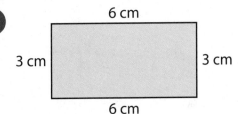 6 cm, 3 cm, 3 cm, 6 cm

3 A rectangle with length 9 inches and width 6 inches.

4 A square with sides 8 feet.

5 A rectangle with length 5 meters and width 4 meters.

6 A rectangle with length 8 meters and width 1 meter.

Set 8: Solve Two-Step Word Problems

Solve the problems. Show your work.

1 Granola bars come in boxes of 5. In a cupboard, there are 2 shelves with 4 full boxes of granola bars on each shelf. How many granola bars are in the cupboard?

2 Students in the art club raise $72 for art supplies. They spend $30 on paper. They want to spend the rest of the money on paint. Each color of paint costs $6. How many colors of paint can they buy?

3 A baker made 115 cookies. He packs 7 boxes with 10 cookies each. The rest of the cookies are not in boxes. How many cookies are not in boxes?

Set 9: Use Order and Grouping to Multiply

Fill in the blanks.

1 $3 \times 7 = 7 \times$ ....

2 $9 \times 4 =$ .... $\times 9$

3 $(3 \times 3) \times 3 = 9 \times$ ....

4 $4 \times 2 \times 5 = 4 \times$ ....

5 $8 \times 3 \times 2 =$ .... $\times 8 \times 3$

6 $4 \times 8 = 4 \times ($ .... $\times 4)$

7 $(4 \times$ .... $) \times 6 = 4 \times (6 \times 5)$

8 .... $\times 3 \times 2 = 7 \times 6$

Cumulative Practice

Name: _____

Set 1: Time

Write the time in two ways in problems 1 and 2.

1

....

.... minutes before ....

2

....

.... minutes after ....

Solve problem 3. Show your work.

3 Steve's soccer game starts at 5:30 PM. Steve wants to be at the field 20 minutes before the game starts. It takes him 8 minutes to get to the field. What time should Steve leave home?

Set 2: Liquid Volume

Solve the problems. Show your work.

1 Alvaro uses a 5-liter watering can to water his flowers. He fills the watering can 6 times and uses all the water. How much water does Alvaro use to water his flowers?

2 A water truck can hold 375 liters of water. There are 165 liters of water in the truck. How much more water can the truck hold?

Set 3: Mass

Solve the problems. Show your work.

1 Ami buys some 3-kilogram bags of apples. In total, she has 9 kilograms of apples. How many bags of apples does she buy?

2 Kellan has a cat and a dog. The dog's mass is 30 kilograms. The cat's mass is 5 kilograms. What is the difference in mass between the cat and the dog?

3 Joe carries a book and a pencil. The book's mass is 360 grams. The pencil's mass is 8 grams. What is the total mass of the book and the pencil?

4 Olive has 10 marbles. Each marble has a mass of 4 grams. What is the total mass of her marbles?

Set 4: Fractions on a Number Line

Identify the fractions at each letter on the number lines for problems 1 and 2.

1

A is ....

2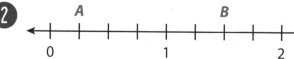

A is ....   B is ....

Label the fraction on the number line for problems 3 and 4.

3 Write $\frac{1}{6}$.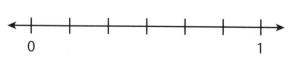

4 Write $\frac{5}{3}$.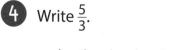

Name: _____

Set 5: Equivalent Fractions

Fill in the missing numbers to make equivalent fractions.

1 $\frac{2}{4} = \frac{\square}{2}$

2 $\frac{2}{3} = \frac{4}{\square}$

3 $\frac{3}{4} = \frac{\square}{8}$

4 $\frac{8}{8} = \frac{\square}{6}$

5 $\frac{1}{4} = \frac{\square}{8}$

6 $\frac{2}{6} = \frac{1}{\square}$

7 $\frac{1}{2} = \frac{4}{\square}$

8 $\frac{1}{2} = \frac{3}{\square}$

9 $\frac{3}{2} = \frac{\square}{4}$

Set 6: Compare Fractions

Write <, >, or = in each circle to compare the fractions.

1 $\frac{2}{3} \bigcirc \frac{2}{4}$

2 $\frac{2}{6} \bigcirc \frac{3}{6}$

3 $\frac{4}{8} \bigcirc \frac{4}{6}$

4 $\frac{1}{2} \bigcirc \frac{1}{2}$

5 $\frac{3}{4} \bigcirc \frac{3}{8}$

6 $\frac{5}{8} \bigcirc \frac{7}{8}$

7 $\frac{3}{4} \bigcirc \frac{1}{4}$

8 $\frac{3}{6} \bigcirc \frac{4}{6}$

9 $\frac{1}{2} \bigcirc \frac{1}{3}$

Set 7: Add Area

Find the total area of each rectangle. Show your work.

1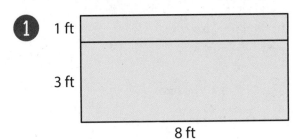
1 ft, 3 ft, 8 ft

2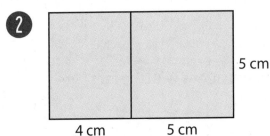
5 cm, 4 cm, 5 cm

Set 8: Multiply

Multiply to solve the problems. Show your work.

1 A teacher gives 4 students 3 stickers each. How many stickers does he give in total?

2 John buys 4 boxes of pencils. Each box has 5 pencils. How many pencils does John buy?

3 Bianca reads 6 chapters. Each chapter has 9 pages. How many pages does she read?

4 A baker makes 8 pies. She uses 7 apples in each pie. How many apples does the baker use in total?

Set 9: Multiplication and Division Facts

Complete the fact families.

1 Write four equations for the fact family with the numbers 5, 7, and 35.

.... $\times$ .... $=$ .... $\div$ .... $=$ ....

.... $\times$ .... $=$ .... $\div$ .... $=$ ....

2 Write four equations with the fact family for $\square \div 4 = 8$.

.... $\times$ .... $=$ .... $\div$ .... $=$ ....

.... $\times$ .... $=$ .... $\div$ .... $=$ ....

3 Write four equations with the fact family for $6 \times \square = 48$.

.... $\times$ .... $=$ .... $\div$ .... $=$ ....

.... $\times$ .... $=$ .... $\div$ .... $=$ ....

Glossary/Glosario

English	Español	Example/Ejemplo

Aa

English	Español	Example/Ejemplo
add to combine or find the total of two or more quantities.	**sumar** combinar o hallar el total de dos o más cantidades.	147 + 212 359
addend a number being added.	**sumando** número que se suma.	$4 + 7 = 11$ addends
algorithm a set of routine steps used to solve problems.	**algoritmo** conjunto de pasos que se siguen rutinariamente para resolver problemas.	1 1 4 5 6 + 1 6 7 6 2 3
AM the time from midnight until before noon.	**a. m.** el tiempo que transcurre desde la medianoche hasta el mediodía.	AM 7:20
analog clock a clock that uses hour and minute hand positions to show time.	**reloj analógico** reloj que muestra la hora con una manecilla de la hora y un minutero.	hour hand / minute hand
angle one of the corners of a shape where two sides meet.	**ángulo** una de las esquinas de una figura en la que se unen dos lados.	angle
area the amount of space inside a closed two-dimensional figure. Area is measured in square units such as square centimeters.	**área** cantidad de espacio dentro de una figura bidimensional cerrada. El área se mide en unidades cuadradas, como los centímetros cuadrados.	Area = 4 square units
array a set of objects arranged in equal rows and equal columns.	**matriz** conjunto de objetos agrupados en filas y columnas iguales.	☆☆☆☆☆ ☆☆☆☆☆ ☆☆☆☆☆

English	Español	Example/Ejemplo
associative property of addition when the grouping of three or more addends is changed, the total does not change.	**propiedad asociativa de la suma** cambiar la agrupación de tres o más sumandos no cambia el total.	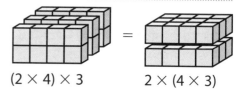 $(2 + 3) + 4 = 2 + (3 + 4)$
associative property of multiplication changing the grouping of three or more factors does not change the product.	**propiedad asociativa de la multiplicación** cambiar la agrupación de tres o más factores no cambia el producto.	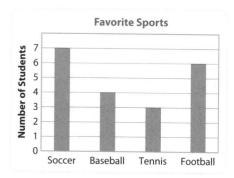 $(2 \times 4) \times 3 \qquad 2 \times (4 \times 3)$
attribute any characteristic of an object or shape, such as number of sides or angles, lengths of sides, or angle measures.	**atributo** característica de un objeto o una figura, como el número de lados o ángulos, la longitud de los lados, o la medida de los ángulos.	attributes of a square: • 4 square corners • 4 sides of equal length

Bb

bar graph a data display in which bars are used to show the number of items in each category.	**gráfica de barras** representación de datos en la cual se usan barras para mostrar el número de elementos de cada categoría.	

Cc

capacity the amount a container can hold. Capacity can be measured in the same units as liquid volume.	**capacidad** cantidad que cabe en un recipiente. La capacidad se mide en las mismas unidades que el volumen líquido.	

capacity of 2 liters

English	Español	Example/Ejemplo
cent (¢) the smallest unit of money in the U.S. One penny has a value of 1 cent. 100 cents is equal to 1 dollar.	**centavo (¢)** la menor unidad monetaria de Estados Unidos. 100 centavos equivalen a 1 dólar.	1 cent 1¢
centimeter (cm) a unit of length. There are 100 centimeters in 1 meter.	**centímetro (cm)** unidad de longitud. 100 centímetros equivalen a 1 metro.	Your little finger is about 1 **centimeter** (cm) across.
column a vertical line of objects or numbers, such as in an array or table.	**columna** línea vertical de objetos o números, como las de una matriz o una tabla.	
commutative property of addition changing the order of addends does not change the total.	**propiedad conmutativa de la suma** cambiar el orden de los sumandos no cambia el total.	$3 + 4 \quad = \quad 4 + 3$
commutative property of multiplication changing the order of the factors does not change the product.	**propiedad conmutativa de la multiplicación** cambiar el orden de los factores no cambia el producto.	$3 \times 2 \quad = \quad 2 \times 3$
compare to decide if numbers, amounts, or sizes are greater than, less than, or equal to each other.	**comparar** determinar si un número, una cantidad, o un tamaño es mayor que, menor que o igual a otro número, otra cantidad u otro tamaño.	$\frac{4}{6} < \frac{5}{6}$

English	Español	Example/Ejemplo
customary system the measurement system commonly used in the United States that measures length in inches, feet, yards, and miles; liquid volume in cups, pints, quarts, and gallons; and weight in ounces and pounds.	**sistema usual** sistema de medición comúnmente usado en Estados Unidos. La longitud se mide en pulgadas, pies, yardas, y millas; el volumen líquido en tazas, pintas, cuartos, y galones; y el peso, en onzas y libras.	**Length** 1 foot = 12 inches 1 yard = 3 feet 1 mile = 5,280 feet **Weight** 1 pound = 16 ounces **Liquid Volume** 1 quart = 2 pints 1 quart = 4 cups 1 gallon = 4 quarts

Dd

English	Español	Example/Ejemplo
data a set of collected information. Often numerical information such as a list of measurements.	**datos** conjunto de información reunida. A menudo es información numérica, tal como una lista de mediciones.	Number of points scored Alan: 2, Cate: 6, Gary: 10, Mae: 8
denominator the number below the line in a fraction that tells the number of equal parts in the whole.	**denominador** número que está debajo de la línea de una fracción. Dice cuántas partes iguales hay en el entero.	$\frac{2}{3}$
difference the result of subtraction.	**diferencia** el resultado de la resta.	$\begin{array}{r} 475 \\ -296 \\ \hline 179 \end{array}$
digit a symbol used to write numbers.	**dígito** símbolo que se usa para escribir números.	The digits are 0, 1, 2, 3, 4, 5, 6, 7, 8, and 9.
digital clock a clock that uses digits to show the time.	**reloj digital** reloj que usa dígitos para mostrar la hora.	AM 7:20

English	Español	Example/Ejemplo
dime a coin with a value of 10 cents (10¢).	**moneda de 10¢** moneda con un valor de 10 centavos (10¢).	10 cents 10¢
dimension length in one direction. A figure may have one, two, or three dimensions.	**dimensión** longitud en una dirección. Una figura puede tener una, dos, o tres dimensiones.	5 in. 2 in. 3 in.
distributive property when one of the factors of a product is written as a sum, multiplying each addend by the other factor before adding does not change the product.	**propiedad distributiva** cuando uno de los factores de un producto se escribe como suma, multiplicar cada sumando por el otro factor antes de sumar no cambia el producto.	$2 \times (3 + 6) = (2 \times 3) + (2 \times 6)$
divide to separate into equal groups and find the number in each group or the number of groups.	**dividir** separar en grupos iguales y hallar cuántos hay en cada grupo o el número de grupos.	15 balloons 5 groups of 3 balloons
dividend the number that is divided by another number.	**dividendo** el número que se divide por otro número.	$15 \div 3 = 5$
division an operation used to separate a number of items into equal-sized groups.	**división** operación que se usa para separar una cantidad de elementos en grupos iguales.	**Division** $12 \div 3 = 4$ total number of groups number in each group
division equation an equation with a divison symbol and an equal sign.	**ecuación de división** ecuación que contiene un signo de división y un signo de igual.	$15 \div 3 = 5$

English	Español	Example/Ejemplo
divisor the number by which another number is divided.	**divisor** el número por el que se divide otro número.	$15 \div 3 = 5$
dollar ($) a unit of money in the U.S. There are 100 cents in 1 dollar ($1).	**dólar ($)** unidad monetaria de Estados Unidos. Un dólar ($1) equivale a 100 centavos.	

Ee

English	Español	Example/Ejemplo
edge a line segment where two faces meet in a three-dimensional shape.	**arista** segmento de recta donde se encuentran dos caras de una figura tridimensional.	Edge
elapsed time the amount of time that has passed between a start time and an end time.	**tiempo transcurrido** tiempo que ha pasado entre el momento de inicio y el fin.	The elapsed time from 2:00 PM to 3:00 PM is 1 hour.
equal having the same value, same size, or same amount.	**igual** que tiene el mismo valor, el mismo tamaño, o la misma cantidad.	$25 + 15 = 40$ $25 + 15$ **is equal to** 40.
equal sign (=) a symbol that means *is the same value as*.	**signo de igual (=)** símbolo que significa *tiene el mismo valor que*.	$12 + 4 = 16$
equation a mathematical statement that uses an equal sign (=) to show that two expressions have the same value.	**ecuación** enunciado matemático en el que se usa un signo de igual (=) para mostrar que dos expresiones tienen el mismo valor.	$25 - 15 = 10$

English	Español	Example/Ejemplo
equivalent fractions two or more different fractions that name the same part of a whole or the same point on a number line.	**fracciones equivalentes** dos o más fracciones diferentes que nombran la misma parte de un entero y el mismo punto de una recta numérica.	$\frac{2}{4} = \frac{1}{2}$ $\frac{5}{10} = \frac{1}{2}$
estimate (noun) a close guess made using mathematical thinking.	**estimación** suposición aproximada que se hace usando el razonamiento matemático.	$28 + 21 = ?$ $30 + 20 = 50$ 50 is an estimate of the sum.
estimate (verb) to make a close guess based on mathematical thinking.	**estimar / hacer una estimación** hacer una suposición aproximada usando el razonamiento matemático.	$28 + 21$ is about 50.
even number a whole number that always has 0, 2, 4, 6, or 8 in the ones place. An even number of objects can be put into pairs or into two equal groups without any leftovers.	**número par** número entero que siempre tiene 0, 2, 4, 6, o 8 en la posición de las unidades. Un número par de objetos puede agruparse en pares o en dos grupos iguales sin que queden sobrantes.	20, 22, 24, 26, and 28 are even numbers.
expanded form the way a number is written to show the place value of each digit.	**forma desarrollada** manera de escribir un número para mostrar el valor posicional de cada dígito.	$249 = 200 + 40 + 9$
expression one or more numbers, unknown numbers, and/or operation symbols that represents a quantity.	**expresión** uno o más números, números desconocidos o símbolos de operaciones que representan una cantidad.	3×4 or $5 + b$

English	Español	Example/Ejemplo

Ff

English	Español	Example/Ejemplo
face a flat surface of a solid shape.	**cara** superficie plana de una figura sólida.	← face
fact family a group of related equations that use the same numbers, but in a different order, and two different operation symbols. A fact family can show the relationship between addition and subtraction or between multiplication and division.	**familia de datos** grupo de ecuaciones relacionadas que tienen los mismos números, ordenados de distinta manera, y dos símbolos de operaciones diferentes. Una familia de datos puede mostrar la relación que existe entre la suma y la resta.	$5 \times 4 = 20$ $4 \times 5 = 20$ $20 \div 4 = 5$ $20 \div 5 = 4$
factor a number that is multiplied.	**factor** número que se multiplica.	$4 \times 5 = 20$ factors
foot (ft) a unit of length in the customary system. There are 12 inches in 1 foot.	**pie (ft)** unidad de longitud del sistema usual. 1 pie equivale a 12 pulgadas.	12 inches = 1 foot
fourths the parts formed when a whole is divided into four equal parts.	**cuartos** partes que se forman cuando se divide un entero de cuatro partes iguales.	fourths 4 equal parts
fraction a number that names equal parts of a whole. A fraction names a point on the number line.	**fracción** número que nombra partes iguales de un entero. Una fracción nombra un punto en una recta numérica.	$\dfrac{3}{4}$

English	Español	Example/Ejemplo

Gg

gram (g) a unit of mass in the metric system. A paper clip has a mass of about 1 gram. There are 1,000 grams in 1 kilogram.	**gramo (g)** unidad de masa del sistema métrico. Un clip tiene una masa de aproximadamente 1 gramo. 1,000 gramos equivalen a 1 kilogramo.	1,000 grams = 1 kilogram
greater than symbol (>) a symbol used to compare two numbers when the first is greater than the second.	**símbolo de mayor que (>)** símbolo que se usa para comparar dos números cuando el primero es mayor que el segundo.	$\frac{1}{2} > \frac{1}{4}$

Hh

halves the parts formed when a whole is divided into two equal parts.	**medios** partes que se obtienen cuando se divide un entero en dos partes iguales.	halves 2 equal parts
hexagon a two-dimensional closed shape with 6 straight sides and 6 corners.	**hexágono** figura bidimensional cerrada que tiene 6 lados y 6 ángulos.	
hour (h) a unit of time. There are 60 minutes in 1 hour.	**hora (h)** unidad de tiempo. 1 hora equivale a 60 minutos.	60 minutes = 1 hour
hour hand the shorter hand on a clock. It shows the hours.	**manecilla de la hora** la manecilla más corta de un reloj. Muestra las horas.	hour hand

English	Español	Example/Ejemplo

Ii

inch (in.) a unit of length in the customary system. There are 12 inches in 1 foot.

pulgada (pulg.) unidad de longitud del sistema usual. 12 pulgadas equivalen a 1 pie.

The length of a quarter is about 1 **inch** (in.).

Kk

key tells what each symbol in a picture graph represents.

clave dice qué representa cada símbolo de una pictografía.

Points Scored During the Game

Alan	🏀
Cate	🏀🏀🏀
Gary	🏀🏀🏀🏀🏀
Mae	🏀🏀🏀🏀

Key: Each stands for 2 points.

↑
Key

kilogram (kg) a unit of mass in the metric system. There are 1,000 grams in 1 kilogram.

kilogramo (kg) unidad de masa del sistema métrico. Un kilogramo equivale a 1,000 gramos.

1,000 grams = 1 kilogram

Ll

length measurement that tells the distance from one point to another, or how long something is.

longitud medida que indica la distancia de un punto a otro, o cuán largo es un objeto.

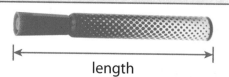

length

English	Español	Example/Ejemplo
less than symbol (<) a symbol used to compare two numbers when the first is less than the second.	**símbolo de menor que (<)** símbolo que se usa para comparar dos números cuando el primero es menor que el segundo.	$\frac{1}{4} < \frac{1}{2}$
line plot a data display that shows data as marks above a number line.	**diagrama de puntos** representación de datos en la cual se muestran los datos como marcas sobre una recta numérica.	**Sea Lion Lengths** x x x x x x x x ←─┼──┼──┼──┼──┼─→ 48 49 50 51 52 **Inches**
liquid volume the amount of space a liquid takes up.	**volumen líquido** cantidad de espacio que ocupa un líquido.	When you measure how much water is in a bucket, you measure liquid volume.
liter (L) a unit of liquid volume in the metric system. There are 1,000 milliliters in 1 liter.	**litro (l)** unidad de volumen líquido del sistema métrico. Un litro equivale a 1,000 mililitros.	1,000 milliliters = 1 liter

Mm

English	Español	Example/Ejemplo
mass the amount of matter in an object. Measuring the mass of an object is one way to measure how heavy it is. Units of mass include the gram and kilogram.	**masa** la cantidad de materia que hay en un objeto. Medir la masa de un objeto es una manera de medir qué tan pesado es. Las unidades de masa incluyen el gramo y el kilogramo.	The mass of a paper clip is about 1 gram.
measure to find length, height, or weight by comparing it to a known unit.	**medir** determinar la longitud, la altura o el peso de un objeto comparándolo con una unidad conocida.	

English	Español	Example/Ejemplo
meter (m) a unit of length in the metric system. There are 100 centimeters in 1 meter.	**metro (m)** unidad de longitud del sistema métrico. 1 metro es igual a 100 centímetros.	100 centimeters = 1 meter
metric system the measurement system that measures length based on meters, liquid volume based on liters, and mass based on grams.	**sistema métrico** sistema de medición. La longitud se mide en metros; el volumen líquido, en litros; y la masa, en gramos.	**Length** 1 kilometer = 1,000 meters 1 meter = 100 centimeters 1 meter = 1,000 millimeters **Mass** 1 kilogram = 1,000 grams **Volume** 1 Liter = 1,000 milliliters
minute (min) a unit of time. There are 60 minutes in 1 hour.	**minuto (min)** unidad de tiempo. 60 minutos equivalen a 1 hora.	60 minutes = 1 hour
minute hand the longer hand on a clock. It shows minutes.	**minutero** la manecilla más larga de un reloj. Muestra los minutos.	minute hand
mixed number a number with a whole-number part and a fractional part.	**número mixto** número con una parte entera y una parte fraccionaria.	$2\frac{3}{8}$
multiplication an operation used to find the total number of items in a given number of equal-sized groups.	**multiplicación** operación que se usa para hallar el número total de objetos en un número dado de grupos de igual tamaño.	**3 groups** of **2 balls** is **6**. $3 \times 2 = 6$
multiplication equation an equation with a multiplication symbol and an equal sign.	**ecuación de multiplicación** ecuación que contiene un signo de multiplicación y un signo de igual.	$3 \times 5 = 15$

English	Español	Example/Ejemplo
multiplication table a table showing multiplication facts.	**tabla de multiplicación** tabla que muestra multiplicaciones y sus resultados.	<table><tr><td></td><td>0</td><td>1</td><td>2</td><td>3</td><td>4</td><td>5</td></tr><tr><td>0</td><td>0</td><td>0</td><td>0</td><td>0</td><td>0</td><td>0</td></tr><tr><td>1</td><td>0</td><td>1</td><td>2</td><td>3</td><td>4</td><td>5</td></tr><tr><td>2</td><td>0</td><td>2</td><td>4</td><td>6</td><td>8</td><td>10</td></tr><tr><td>3</td><td>0</td><td>3</td><td>6</td><td>9</td><td>12</td><td>15</td></tr><tr><td>4</td><td>0</td><td>4</td><td>8</td><td>12</td><td>16</td><td>20</td></tr><tr><td>5</td><td>0</td><td>5</td><td>10</td><td>15</td><td>20</td><td>25</td></tr></table>
multiply to repeatedly add the same number a certain number of times. Used to find the total number of items in equal-sized groups.	**multiplicar** sumar el mismo número una y otra vez una cierta cantidad de veces. Se multiplica para hallar el número total de objetos que hay en grupos de igual tamaño.	42 36 30 24 18 12 6 $7 \times 6 = 42$

Nn

English	Español	Example/Ejemplo
nickel a coin with a value of 5 cents (5¢).	**moneda de 5¢** moneda con un valor de 5 centavos (5¢).	5 cents 5¢
number line a straight line marked at equal spaces to show numbers.	**recta numérica** recta que tiene marcas separadas por espacios iguales; las marcas muestran números.	0 1 2 3 4
numerator the number above the line in a fraction that tells the number of equal parts that are being described.	**numerador** número que está encima de la línea de una fracción. Dice cuántas partes iguales se describen.	$\dfrac{2}{3}$

Oo

English	Español	Example/Ejemplo
odd number a whole number that always has 1, 3, 5, 7, or 9 in the ones place. An odd number of objects cannot be put into pairs or into two equal groups without a leftover.	**número impar** número entero que siempre tiene el dígito 1, 3, 5, 7, o 9 en la posición de las unidades. Los números impares no pueden ordenarse en pares o en dos grupos iguales sin que queden sobrantes.	21, 23, 25, 27, and 29 are odd numbers.

English	Español	Example/Ejemplo
operation a mathematical action such as addition, subtraction, multiplication, or division.	**operación** acción matemática como la suma, la resta, la multiplicación, y la división.	$15 + 5 = 20$ $20 - 5 = 15$ $4 \times 6 = 24$ $24 \div 6 = 4$

Pp

English	Español	Example/Ejemplo
parallel always the same distance apart.	**paralelos** que siempre están a la misma distancia.	
parallelogram a quadrilateral with opposite sides parallel and equal in length.	**paralelogramo** cuadrilátero con lados opuestos paralelos e iguales en longitud.	
partial sums the sums you get in each step of the partial-sums strategy. You use place value to find partial sums.	**sumas parciales** las sumas que se obtienen en cada paso de la estrategia de sumas parciales. Se usa el valor posicional para hallar sumas parciales.	The partial sums for $124 + 234$ are $100 + 200$ or 300, $20 + 30$ or 50, and $4 + 4$ or 8.
partial-sums strategy a strategy used to add multi-digit numbers.	**estrategia de sumas parciales** estrategia que se usa para sumar números de varios dígitos.	312 $+ 235$ **Add the hundreds.** 500 **Add the tens.** 40 **Add the ones.** $+ \ \ 7$ 547
pattern a series of numbers or shapes that follow a rule to repeat or change.	**patrón** serie de números o figuras que siguen una regla para repetirse o cambiar.	
penny a coin with a value of 1 cent (1¢).	**moneda de un 1¢** moneda con un valor de 1 centavo (1¢).	1 cent 1¢
pentagon a two-dimensional closed shape with exactly 5 sides and 5 angles.	**pentágono** figura bidimensional cerrada que tiene exactamente 5 lados y 5 ángulos.	

English	Español	Example/Ejemplo
perimeter the distance around a two-dimensional shape. The perimeter is equal to the sum of the lengths of the sides.	**perímetro** longitud del contorno de una figura bidimensional. El perímetro es igual al total de las longitudes de los lados.	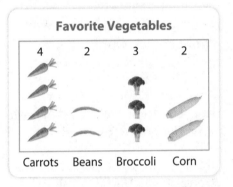 The perimeter of the soccer field is 200 yards. (60 yd + 40 yd + 60 yd + 40 yd)
picture graph a data display in which pictures are used to show data.	**pictografía** representación de datos en la cual se usan dibujos para mostrar datos.	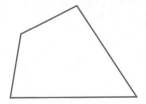
place value the value assigned to a digit based on its position in a number.	**valor posicional** valor de un dígito según su posición en un número.	
PM the time from noon until before midnight.	**p. m.** tiempo desde el mediodía hasta la medianoche.	PM 5:10
product the result of multiplication.	**producto** el resultado de la multiplicación.	5 × 3 = 15

Qq

quadrilateral a two-dimensional closed shape with exactly 4 sides and 4 angles.	**cuadrilátero** figura bidimensional cerrada que tiene exactamente 4 lados y 4 ángulos.	

English	Español	Example/Ejemplo
quarter a coin with a value of 25 cents (25¢).	**moneda de 25¢** moneda con un valor de 25 centavos (25¢).	25 cents 25¢
quotient the result of division.	**cociente** el resultado de la división.	$15 \div 3 = 5$

Rr

English	Español	Example/Ejemplo
rectangle a quadrilateral with 4 right angles. Opposite sides of a rectangle are the same length.	**rectángulo** paralelogramo que tiene 4 ángulos rectos. Los lados opuestos de un rectángulo tienen la misma longitud.	
regroup to put together or break apart ones, tens, or hundreds.	**reagrupar** unir o separar unidades, decenas, o centenas.	10 ones can be regrouped as 1 ten, or 1 hundred can be regrouped as 10 tens.
rhombus a quadrilateral with all sides the same length.	**rombo** cuadrilátero cuyos lados tienen todos la misma longitud.	
right angle an angle that looks like the corner of a square.	**ángulo recto** ángulo que parece la esquina de un cuadrado.	90°
round to find a number that is close in value to a given number by finding the nearest ten, hundred, or other place value.	**redondear** hallar un número que es cercano en valor al número dado hallando la decena, la centena, o otro valor posicional más cercano.	48 rounded to the nearest ten is 50.
row a horizontal line of objects or numbers, such as in an array or table.	**fila** línea horizontal de objetos o números, tal como las que aparecen en una matriz o una tabla.	

English	Español	Example/Ejemplo
rule a set way that is followed to go from one number or shape to the next in a pattern.	**regla** procedimiento que se sigue para ir de un número o una figura al número o la figura siguiente de un patrón.	17, 22, 27, 32, 37, 42 rule: add 5

Ss

English	Español	Example/Ejemplo
scale (on a graph) the value represented by the distance between one tickmark and the next on a number line.	**escala (en una gráfica)** el valor que representa la distancia entre una marca y la marca siguiente de una recta numérica.	Points Scored During the Game Students: Alan, Cate, Gary, Mae Number of Points Scored: 0 2 4 6 8
second (s) a unit of time. There are 60 seconds in 1 minute.	**segundo (s)** unidad de tiempo. 60 segundos equivalen a 1 minuto.	60 seconds = 1 minute
side a line segment that forms part of a two-dimensional shape.	**lado** segmento de recta que forma parte de una figura bidimensional.	side
square a quadrilateral with 4 square corners and 4 sides of equal length.	**cuadrado** cuadrilátero que tiene 4 esquinas cuadradas y 4 lados de igual longitud.	
square unit the area of a square with side lengths of 1 unit.	**unidad cuadrada** el área de un cuadrado que tiene lados de 1 unidad de longitud.	1 unit 1 unit 1 unit 1 unit
subtract to take away one quantity from another, or to compare two numbers to find the difference.	**restar** quitar una cantidad a otra, o comparar dos números para hallar la diferencia.	365 − 186 = 179

English	Español	Example/Ejemplo
sum the result of addition.	**suma** el resultado de la suma.	$34 + 25 = 59$

Tt

English	Español	Example/Ejemplo
thirds the parts formed when a whole is divided into three equal parts.	**tercios** partes que se forman cuando se divide un entero en tres partes iguales.	thirds 3 equal parts
three-dimensional solid, or having length, width, and height. For example, a cube is three-dimensional.	**tridimensional** sólido, o que tiene longitud, ancho, y altura. Por ejemplo, los cubos son tridimensionales.	
trapezoid (exclusive) a quadrilateral with exactly one pair of parallel sides.	**trapecio** cuadrilátero que tiene exactamente un par de lados paralelos.	
trapezoid (inclusive) a quadrilateral with at least one pair of parallel sides.	**trapecio** cuadrilátero que tiene al menos un par de lados paralelos.	
triangle a two-dimensional closed shape with exactly 3 sides and 3 angles.	**triángulo** figura bidimensional cerrada que tiene exactamente 3 lados y 3 ángulos.	
two-dimensional flat, or having measurement in two directions, like length and width. For example, a rectangle is two-dimensional.	**bidimensional** plano, o que tiene medidas en dos direcciones, como la longitud y el ancho. Por ejemplo, un rectángulo es bidimensional.	

English	Español	Example/Ejemplo

Uu

English	Español	Example/Ejemplo
unit fraction a fraction with a numerator of 1. Other fractions are built from unit fractions.	**fracción unitaria** fracción cuyo numerador es 1. Otras fracciones se construyen a partir de fracciones unitarias.	$\frac{1}{4}$

Vv

English	Español	Example/Ejemplo
vertex the point where two rays, lines, or line segments meet to form an angle.	**vértice** punto donde dos semirrectas, rectas, o segmentos de recta se unen y forman un ángulo.	Vertex

Yy

English	Español	Example/Ejemplo
yard (yd) a unit of length in the customary system. There are 3 feet, or 36 inches, in 1 yard.	**yarda (yd)** unidad de longitud del sistema usual de Estados Unidos. 1 yarda equivale a 3 pies o a 36 pulgadas.	3 feet = 1 yard 36 inches = 1 yard

Acknowledgments

Common Core State Standards © 2010. National Governors Association Center for Best Practices and Council of Chief State School Officers. All rights reserved.

Photography Credits

United States coin images (unless otherwise indicated) from the United States Mint

Images used under license from **Shutterstock.com**.

iii ArtMari, lendy16; **iv** Dimedrol68; **v** akiyoko, Vadim; **vi** Artismo, Hurst Photo, Rashad Ashurov, trekandshoot; **vii** sumire8, TerryM; **viii** CyrilLutz, Kaiskynet; **1** Kristina Vackova; **3** Erica Truex, Iraidka; **4** En min Shen, Erica Truex; **9** Erica Truex, Seregam; **10** Billion Photos, Erica Truex, EtiAmmos; **13** Erica Truex, Ralko; **14** blue67design, Erica Truex, Jagodka, LHF Graphics, Nina_Susik; **15** Edwin Verin, Erica Truex, palform; **16** Erica Truex, palform, Rich Koele; **19** Bogdan ionescu, Erica Truex; **20** Northallertonman; **23** Erica Truex, GOLFX, Lightspring; **24** Lane V. Erickson; **27** likekightcm; **30** Erica Truex, Javier Brosch, RomanJuve; **31** Erica Truex, Fabio Berti, palform; **34** Dudarev Mikhail, Erica Truex; **40** Erica Truex, S-ts; **41** Erica Truex, Gavrylovaphoto, palform; **42** Erica Truex, Kithanet, palform; **45** Andrey Lobachev, Art'nLera, olllikeballoon; **49** pattara puttiwong; **52** Dima Sobko; **53** IROOM STOCK, palform; **54** palform, studiolovin; **56** PhotoProCorp; **57** Federico Quevedo; **58** Erica Truex, palform, Plumdesign; **59** Erica Truex, Shebeko; **60** Ed Samuel, Erica Truex; **61** Erica Truex, Kzww; **62** Erica Truex, lendy16; **69** AfricaStudio, Erica Truex; **70** Erica Truex, Natu, palform; **74** Stephen Orsillo; **75** Cmnaumann, palform; **76** Dangdumrong, otsphoto; **80** Triff; **81** SeDmi, smilewithjul; **82** David Franklin; **83** Wsantina; **89** Shuter; **91** Kovalchuk Oleksandr, Kyselova Inna; **92** Pete Spiro, Photosync; **93** KK Tan; **96** Petlia Roman; **97** Rose Carson; **99** Fotofermer, Irin-k; **100** freestyle images; **101** Tim UR; **102** Pete Spiro; **105** Pets in frames; **108** Timothy Boomer; **109–110** charles taylor; **112** Coprid, marssanya; **113** M. Unal Ozmen, Maks Narodenko; **114** Mario7, Tim UR; **116** Elnur, Lubava; **119** CrackerClips Stock Media; **120** Studio DMM Photography, Designs & Art; **122** SOMMAI; **125** Lubava, Valentina Razumova; **126** Jiri Hera, showcake, Stockforlife, Vitaly Zorkin; **127–128** Valentina Rozumova; **130** Viacheslav Rubel; **131** Natasha Pankina, SUN-FLOWER; **132** Hannamariah, marssanya; **134** Iriskana, Photo Melon; **136** Le Do, liskus; **137–138** Aopsan, Claudio Divizia; **141** Sashkin; **143** AS Food studio, smilewithjul; **144** AS Food studio; **147** Lukas Gojda, Valentina Proskurina; **148** Yaping; **149** Kyselova Inna, Triff; **150** KMNPhoto; **152** Elena Schweitzer, Iriskana; **153** Lifestyle Graphic; **154** Tropper2000; **159** Dimedrol68; **160** Dimedrol68, liskus, SOMMAI; **163** Danny Smythe; **164** normallens; **165–166** Tadeusz Wejkszo; **169** Andrea Izzotti, Celso Diniz, Chris Bradshaw, Christian Musat, Denton Rumsey, Don Mammoser, f11 photo, FloridaStock, GUDKOV ANDREY, Henryk Sadura, Jason Patrick Ross, Jayne Carney, liquid studios, moosehenderson, Romrodphoto; **171** Rido, smilewithjul; **172** Bajinda, liskus, Maks Narodenko; **174** Elnur, Ksuxa-muxa; **177** Narong Jongsirikul; **179** Alexey D. Vedernikov; **180** Kletr, smilewithjul; **181** ArtMari, Nattika, palform; **182** Claudio Divizia, palform; **183** Africa Studio, palform; **184** Drozhzhina Elena; **186** mayer kleinostheim, palform; **187** palform, Natalia D; **190** Boris Sosnovyy, palform; **192** Africa Studio, palform; **193** palform, Redchocolate, Lenorko; **194** Lenorko, palform, Redchocolate, TerraceStudio; **197** Karkas, Coprid, Olga Popova, palform; **199** stockcreations; **200** Gbuglok, palform; **202** Olga Lyubkin, palform; **207** Erofeeva Natalya, palform; **208** palform, Phase4Studios, Picsfive; **209** ArtnLera, palform, paulaphoto; **211** ajt, palform; **212** ArtnLera, FabrikaSimf, palform; **214** Balabolka, EtiAmmos, monticello, palform; **215** ArtnLera, Cergios, palform; **216** Caimacanul, Design56, Redchocolate; **218** Balabolka, Michelle D. Milliman; **221** Balabolka, Odua Images; **222** palform, Vstock24; **223** Ocram, palform; **224** palform, Vangert; **225** Ivaschenko Roman, palform; **226** Juthamat8899; **227** Andrey_Kuzmin; **228** mr.chanwit wangsuk palform; **230** COLOA Studio, LHF Graphics; **231** Cheers Group, HelgaLin, palform; **233** Anneka, Kschrei, palform, Vesna cvorovic; **234** Denis Pepin, palform; **235** Ivory27; **236** palform, Pao Laroid; **237** nld, Runrun2; **238** HamsterMan, Robyn Mackenzie; **239** Craig Wactor, palform; **240** AlexPic, mohamad firdaus bin ramli; **242** AlexPic, Quang Ho; **243** Natalia7, palform; **245** Bryan Solomon, motorolka, palform; **246** r.classen, palform, Valentina Proskurina; **247** Maria Jeffs; **250** En min Shen; **251** oksana2010; **252** Somboon Bunproy; **254** artnLera, Hong Vo, sevenke, Tiwat K; **255** Shippee; **256** HodagMedia; **259** Kletr; **262** Africa Studio; **264** smilewithjul, Steve Cukrov; **268** Dontree; **272** Jiradet Ponari; **283** palform, Shuter; **286** Vdimage; **289** Alekseykolotvin; **290** Suzanne Tucker; **291** Victor Moussa; **299** JARIRIYAWAT; **303** Kovalenko Dmitriy, Route55; **306** Roman Dick; **314** Gl0ck, Tiwat K; **315** Tom Pavlasek; **318** Undrey; **320** Plufflyman; **322** Irina Fischer; **325** Bragin Alexey; **326** Ksenia Palimski; **329** areeya_ann; **333** Coprid; **334** balabolka, MaxCab; **335** Drozhzhina Elena, palform; **337** Vadim Sadovski; **338** palform; **340** palform, RomanStrela; **341** Fotokostic, Oleg Romanko, VVO; **346** cherezoff, palform; **345–348** akiyoko, palform; **356** artnLera, Dmitry Zimin, En min Shen; **357** artnLera, Olivier Le Queinec; **358** EHStockphoto; **359** Maks Narodenko; Matt Benoit; **360** Pavlo_K; **361** Svetlana Serebryakova, Olga Nikonova; **362** LAURA_VN, Quang Ho; **363** bluehand, Olga Nikonova; **364** Miroslav Halama; **366** LittleMiss, MarGi; **367** lana rinck; **369** Roma Borman; **370** Roma Borman; **372** aquariagirl1970, Tim UR; **373** Africa Studio, Simon Bratt; **374** balabolka, Max Lashcheuski; **375** Madlen; **378** Aopsan, Claudio Divizia, Natasha Pankina; **379** kruraphoto; **380** Ultimax; **383** vikky; **384** palform, YUTTASAK SAMPACHANO; **385** anna. q, Iriskana, Quanthem; **386** Iriskana, ES sarawuth, topform; **387** Surrphoto; **390** BW Folsom; **391** balabolka, Leigh Prather; **392** Lotus_studio; **394** Mauro Rodrigues; **395** Alchena; **396** Andrey Eremin, Iriskana; **397–398** abdrahimmahfar; **400** marre; **402** jannoon028; **403** Aluna1, Pandapaw; **404** Aluna1, Tropper2000; **407** Simic Vojislav; **408** Iriskana, Peshkova; **411** photosync, redchocolate; **412** NinaM; **414** Erica Truex, irin-k; **415** Cherdchai charasri, Erica Truex; **418** CrackerClips Stock Media; **419** Aliaksei Tarasau, Flower Studio, LilKar; **420–421** Aliaksei Tarasau; **422** Aliaksei Tarasau, Smit; **423** Erica Truex, Valdis Skudre; **424** Joshua Lewis, Tiwat K; **425** STILLFX; **426** Chones; **428** Erica Truex, Sergiy Kuzmin; **430** Katstudio, Tiwat K; **431** attapoljochosobig, Iriskana; **432** JUN3, Iriskana; **434** Protasov AN; **435–436** Aliaksei Tarasau; **438** Smileus; **439** David Franklin, Iriskana, palform; **440** irin-k, Iurii Osadchi; **441** Oksana2010; **442, 444** Khvost, Ronald Sumners, Surrphoto; **446** Sergey Chayko; **455** Africa Studio; **457** Hurst Photo; **458** Olga Nayashkova; **462** CKP1001;

Front Cover credits

©Teri Lyn Fisher/Offset